The Gardener's Life

THE GARDENER'S LIFE

Inspired Plantsmen, Passionate Collectors, and Singular Visions in the World of Gardening

LAURENCE SHEEHAN
photographs by WILLIAM STITES

with CAROL SAMA SHEEHAN
and KATHRYN GEORGE PRECOURT

design by DINA DELL'ARCIPRETE
dk DESIGN PARTNERS INC.

CLARKSON POTTER/PUBLISHERS
NEW YORK

Published by Clarkson Potter/Publishers, New York, New York
Member of the Crown Publishing Group, a division of Random House, Inc.
www.crownpublishing.com

CLARKSON N. POTTER is a trademark and POTTER and colophon are
registered trademarks of Random House, Inc.

Printed in China

Library of Congress Cataloging-in-Publication Data
Sheehan, Laurence.
   The gardener's life: inspired plantsmen, passionate collectors, and singular
visions in the world of gardening / Laurence Sheehan; with Carol Sama Sheehan
and Kathryn George Precourt; photographs by William Stites. —1st ed.
1. Gardeners—United States—Anecdotes. 2. Gardens—United States—
Anecdotes. 3. Gardening—United States—Anecdotes. 4. Gardeners—
United States—Pictorial works. 5. Gardens—United States—Pictorial works.
6. Gardening—United States—Pictorial works.   I. Title.
   SB455 .S434   2004
   635'.092'273—dc22   2003017661

ISBN 0-609-60939-4

10   9   8   7   6   5   4   3   2   1

First Edition

CONTENTS

INTRODUCTION

A LIFE IN THE GARDEN

If you should have a lovely garden,

live a lovely life.

—SHAKER SAYING

In spite of good advice from a host of eminent authorities and steady, even gallant, toil on my own part during our growing season, my results in the array of gardens I have built on our old dairy farm in rural western Massachusetts remain mixed. A few years ago, for example, I erected a handsome pergola, using young maples culled from our woods as posts, and planted it up with several varieties of honeysuckle. The vines have matured beautifully, blossoming in shades of yellow and red and hosting ruby-throated hummingbirds and honeybees all summer.

Two sets of brides and grooms have marched down the aisle formed by my pergola, then across a swath of lawn to a makeshift altar that happened to be framed by a profusion of roses and peonies in bloom, as if planting them there had been intended. (June weddings sharply concentrate the gardener's mind.) But now the posts in my pergola have mostly fallen, kneecapped by rot, and in the present winter of my discontent resemble nothing so much as a game of pick-me-up sticks gone amok.

It is one of the ironies of gardening that the garden always remains subordinate to the whims of nature. My calamities in my garden put me in good company: Even the schemes of our most brilliant gardeners are as full of failure and disappointment as they are of joy and fulfillment. Rain or shine, one must simply get on with it. This philosophy seems to be what drives the gardeners featured in this book, and their dogged persistence has inspired me to carry on in the gardener's life as best I can. Next spring, for example, I will replace the maple posts in the pergola with locust, a material likely to outlast me by a hundred years, I have been informed, laughingly, by a neighbor whose family came over on

the *Mayflower.* Or, having had my head turned recently by an ironmonger's interpretation of a pergola in an issue of the British magazine *Gardens Illustrated,* I might opt to have a set of graceful Roman arches made for me out of the crude but durable reinforcing material rebar. As the 19th-century American landscape and garden guru Liberty Hyde Bailey said, in urging gardeners simply to embrace what *is* instead of longing for what is *not,* "The man who worries morning and night about the dandelions in the lawn will find great relief in loving dandelions."

If any single experience shaped my perspective on the challenge of gardening, it was the year I managed a friend's garden center in Westport, Connecticut, in the 1980s. The year of gardening dangerously, as I came to think of it, introduced me to a world of inspired plantsmen and growers like Allen Haskell, whose nursery in New Bedford, Massachusetts, is a mecca for serious gardeners, and Sal Gilbertie, who keeps long farmer's hours for the sake of his plants and his customers. The knowledge and experience of such plantsmen (and plantswomen), as growers, designers, and guides, is an essential ingredient of the gardening life and of this book.

In the course of business I also met artists and craftsmen of singular vision in the gardening world, such as Abbie Zabar of New York City, whose books and gardens reflect a sensibility that is precocious without being precious, both funny and profound, and Guy Wolff, a virtuoso in the medium of wet clay, whose classically shaped pottery, thrown by hand in a tiny shop in Washington, Connecticut, is coveted by gardeners all over the country. Apart from their shared gift of seeing things freshly, artists have cultivated the habit of breaking rules and taking chances, and we can learn from them in giving identity to our own gardening adventures.

Finally, I came to know and admire such passionate collectors as Anne Rowe, a New Hampshire dealer in garden antiquities, whose eye for comely and appropriate garden ornaments and accoutrements helped me understand what would catch the eye of gardeners. Among other things, collectors show how one can bring the delights of the garden into the house in a way that expresses the personal tastes of each gardener.

"Under a total want of demand except for our family table, I am still devoted to the garden," wrote Thomas Jefferson toward the end of his life, famously adding, "But though an old man, I am but a young gardener." The never-ending learning process in a gardener's life is one of the things that can make picking up trug and trowel an unexpected pleasure of a morning, and more often than not the prelude to discovery. As Ashfield's preeminent gardener, Elsa Bakalar, put it in *A Garden of One's Own,* "Every day brings change and new marvels. I experience astonishment, delight, revelation— and always beauty, undemanding beauty. . . . There is nothing to understand but everything to absorb."

Like our area's few remaining full-time farmers, who raise hay, grow Christmas trees, produce maple syrup, and also practice magic and music acts on the side, to stay afloat, Mark Zenick wears many hats. He is head of a local land trust by day, so to speak, a daylily grower by night, and an artist in between. He lives on New Hope Farm in a serene corner of Ashfield called Apple Valley. His daylily fields, a wild clash of colors in summer, flanked by apple and pear trees creaking with fruit in the fall, surround his house on three sides. On the brow of a hill overlooking the lilies of the field is Zenick's studio, built by Mark's own hand to the exact specifications of Henry Thoreau's cabin at Walden

Pond. Zenick might be said to approach daylilies the way Thoreau approached his cash crop in the woods: "What shall I learn of beans or beans of me?"

Another Ashfield resident, Beverly Duncan, teaches art and illustrates books for children, but her true passion is botanical art. Although she grew up in Hawaii and northern California, she turns to the natural environment of western Massachusetts for inspiration in creating her detailed studies of leaves, blossoms, fruits, grasses, and trees. Her paintings have been described as combining "the exactitude of scientific illustration with luminous color and elegant line, to convey the delicacy and transience of natural things." Duncan presents her subjects warts and all. If there's a tear in a leaf or a ladybug on the sunflower, she'll include it in the drawing. Her work is widely collected and has been exhibited in such prestigious venues as the Smithsonian Institution in Washington, D.C., and the Hunt Institution for Botanical Documentation in Pittsburgh.

opposite: A rustic garden trellis fashioned out of twigs and vines by Janice Shields in Lenox, Massachusetts.

Farther west, in the Berkshires resort town of Lenox, Janice Shields has found a livelihood in fashioning rustic trellises, gates, gazebos, arbors, obelisks, and other garden structures from materials harvested in the woods, such as birch, hickory, locust, and bittersweet vine (see opposite page). But in her spare time Janice also conducts aerobic swimming classes for women who wear clothes in the larger sizes, who she believes are often too self-conscious to sign up for conventional fitness programs. And she has been a teacher, dress-shop manager, and auto mechanic.

With my experience selling umpteen varieties of lavender at Gilberties' Garden Center in Connecticut, I was naturally drawn to an annual July occurrence around here called Lavender Day Festival. An intrepid local group of farmers and craftspeople banded together a few years ago to promote the herb as a crop, both for its beauty and its utility. The year I went on the tour I got to see Doris Riley's giant walk-through stone-and-lavender labyrinth, which Doris built by hand in the yard behind her house in Montague. And I saw students at Northfield–Mount Hermon School harvest lavender by the basket and then distill the blossoms into oil for use in aromatherapy. I got lost looking for another festival stop, where they were said to be giving away lavender lemonade.

David Fisher, a man in his mid-twenties from Westchester County in New York, operates a farm cooperative on fertile bottomland acreage alongside the South River in Conway, Ashfield's neighbor to the east. He grows vegetables and herbs for his subscribers, more than fifty local families who pay an annual fee of a few hundred dollars for the opportunity to fill a shopping bag with fresh-picked produce once a week from Memorial Day to Thanksgiving. Even though I grow my own vegetables, I have joined Natural Roots, as the Community Supported Agriculture (CSA) farm is called, in seasons past just to see how much Swiss chard (one of those leafy crops of David's that keeps on producing) I could eat. Actually, I like the idea of supporting a small organic farmer who uses 2,000-pound Belgian horses to turn over his soil and wears a beard designed in Amish country. To make a go of farming, David also juggles a multitude of trades. He supplies produce to local restaurants, sells more produce at a nearby farmer's market every Saturday morning in season, and raises his own pork, grass-fed lamb, and Angus beef for sale. The meat products are paid for on an item-by-item basis, David using a makeshift cashbox to keep checks and bills.

Like any lifestyle, the gardener's life has its rituals—diurnal, seasonal, and annual. There are garden tours in every state, so many that even the most ardent garden tourist could not see them all. Many local institutions have plant sales in the early spring every year—the plant sale at the stately Congregational church in our town features specimens that church members dig up from their own gardens to put on the makeshift sale tables. You have to get there before they drop the crime-scene tape, exactly at 9 A.M., to have a shot at obtaining the unusual or best-looking specimens. In the bargain-basement rush to buy, mistakes are made. Why did I buy so much rue, when I can't stand the smell of that plant? Last year it snowed so hard, I wasn't sure what I was picking out (too many dahlias, it turned out, I learned when I got home).

If the early-spring plant sale in our town marks the beginning of the gardening year, the Cummington Fair in the fall brings the curtain down on the whole catastrophe. Country fairs, struggling to survive in the age of arena football, cineplexes, and video war games, are sometimes forced to offer incongruous side attractions to get people, especially young people, through the gate, such as hot air balloon rides, beauty contests, or traveling menageries of wild animals in such pathetic condition that even PETA would shoot them. The officers of the Hillside Agricultural Society, founded in 1883, have pretty much stuck to their old-fashioned guns in putting on Cummington's main attraction every year, giving us the drama of the ox pull and the draft horse pull (in several weight classes), the lesson in work ethic of the border collie demo, and the inspiration of the 4-H and youth competitions in purebred beef and dairy cattle, sheep, poultry, and rabbits.

A native of Cummington, the poet and influential New York newpaper editor William Cullen Bryant died six years before the town's fair got started. He was a passionate amateur botanist from an early age. Shade maple trees he planted still line some of the roads in town. In Manhattan, he joined forces with fellow editor (*The Horticulturist*) and landscape architect Andrew Jackson Downing to lobby successfully for the creation of Central Park. He became an expert particularly on fruit trees, establishing an impressive orchard on his Long Island estate, Cedarmere. In his later years he bought back his childhood home in Cummington and also his grandfather's old farm, 465 acres in all, and planted fruit and ornamental trees and conifers.

The first use of the word *garden* in the New World apparently came in Capt. John Smith's *Descriptions of New England,* published in 1614, in which he reported observing "sandy cliffes and cliffes of rock, both which we saw so planted with Gardens and Cornefields," evidently a reference to Native American farming practices along the Massachusetts seaboard. The Indians who farmed in those days burned underbrush every year to clear land, then planted corn and beans among the surviving trees; the ashes left by the fire served as fertilizer. These annual burns were also believed to increase game populations, making it easier to hunt.

The Puritans of Massachusetts Bay Colony, disdainful of this technique for managing the land, put in place the more familiar English system of fields and fences, introducing their beloved cows, and later sheep and pigs. At first the early settlers raised corn year after year, until the soil was exhausted, forcing them to push into and subdue fresh land farther west, further displacing native populations not already decimated by the firearms of the newcomers or infectious diseases like smallpox.

opposite: Plant sales to raise money for local causes take place in the northlands in early spring—rain, shine, or snow.

While homesteaders settled the countryside, planting orchards and rectilinear, enclosed fields of corn and other grains, city dwellers gardened avidly in their own fashion. Beginning early in the 18th century, Boston became a veritable rabbit warren of kitchen gardens. "To live and keep house in Boston was to grow a garden," states Peter Benes in a report, *Plants and People,* published in 1995 by the Dublin Seminar for New England Folklife, "and to do so with a particularly enlightened purpose." He estimates that as many as three-quarters of the four thousand households identified on a 1743 map of Boston "grew their own vegetables, salads, berries, and occasional fruits in backyard (or frontyard) kitchen gardens." (The next time such a high percentage of Americans would be hoeing rows was World War II: In 1944 twenty million "victory gardens" produced 44 percent of the vegetables in the United States.) A gardening familiarity permeated every level of society. "Working housewives, heads of households, physicians, justices, clergymen, and governors of colonies devoted themselves to their apple orchards, their asparagus beds, their early marrowfat peas, and their currant bushes," writes Benes.

Some of the larger city gardens were commercial enterprises, such as the one that ran this ad in the *Boston Weekly News-Letter* in July of 1735:

Any person that has a mind to take a Walk in the Garden at the Bottom of the Common, to Eat Currants, shall be kindly Welcome for Six Pence a piece.

By 1770, says Benes, there was "a sizeable number of Boston nurserymen, nurserywomen, and truck-farmers who variously imported, propagated, and cultivated seeds, root-stock, plant-stock, and fresh produce for sale to local householders and estate-keepers." Hand in hand with urbanization, the horticultural industry would become mostly the business of professionals.

The literature of gardening, heretofore imported from England, also became Americanized. One of the first books devoted to flowers, albeit a slender volume of fifty-nine pages, was published in Boston in 1828: *A Treatise on the Cultivation of Ornamental Flowers,* by Roland Green. *The Farmer's Manual,* published in 1819, was one of the earliest how-to books on the broader subject of agriculture. The author, Frederick Butler, graduated from Yale in 1785, after which he taught school in Wethersfield, "Connecticut's Most Ancient Towne," and wrote book after book, including the first textbook on American history. The title page of his *Farmer's Manual* in its myriad of typefaces forms a kind of free-verse ode to homesteading:

THE

FARMER'S MANUAL

BEING

A PLAIN PRACTICAL TREATISE

ON THE ART OF

HUSBANDRY,

DESIGNED

TO PROMOTE AN ACQUAINTANCE

WITH THE

MODERN IMPROVEMENTS

IN

AGRICULTURE,

TOGETHER WITH REMARKS ON

GARDENING,

AND A TREATISE ON THE

MANAGEMENT OF

BEES.

In Butler's time, Wethersfield was the onion capital of the world, shipping out staggering amounts of the pungent Wethersfield red onion, strung up in ropes or stowed in barrels, to the West Indies, England, the Mediterranean, and along the American coast from Nova Scotia to Louisiana. According to the local historical society, about a third of the five hundred people employed in the onion fields were girls or single women. "I've heard tell the most respectable females in Wethersfield, even the farmers' own wives and daughters, are not above working in the onion fields there," observes Charity Strong, a character in a historical novel of the same name, set in the era, by Marguerite Allis. (Charity pulls onions one summer to earn money to pay for singing lessons.) "The fair onion-growers united with their industry a laudable care of their beauty," wrote one British visitor in 1807. "In the field, their dress, which is contrived for protecting them from the sun, often disguises every lineament of the human figure."

In addition to onions, the rich fields of Wethersfield produced wheat, rye, peas, Indian corn, flax for making linen, barley for making beer, corn brooms, and hemp for ropemaking. Of the many seed companies that sprang up in town, one survives: Comstock, Ferre & Co., the oldest continuously operating seed company in the country. It was established in 1820 by James Lockwood Belden as the Wethersfield Seed Company. (Seed and garden catalogs from American nurseries begin appearing with some frequency as early as the 1770s.) The original tin signs adorn the buildings to this day. The company was expanded in 1853 when Franklin Comstock and his son, William, succeeded Belden and were later joined by Henry Ferre. The Comstocks had contact with a Shaker village located in nearby Enfield. William adopted their idea of packing seed in paper envelopes and developed the scroll border still used on their herb packets. To this day store visitors will find the original rows of old oak rocker bins and tin-lined oak drawers holding the firm's seed stock.

Yankee agriculture shifted gears in the first half of the 19th century as more and more farmers gave up raising crops for sheep and the lucrative production of wool, so much so, as Mark Kramer reports in his book *Three Farms: Making Milk, Meat and Money from the American Soil,* that "Boston's supply of fowl, butter, and eggs nearly ceased in 1837 because most farmers had turned to sheep." When the domestic wool market collapsed due to an influx of wool from Europe, "many farm families joined the migration to lands not yet depleted by intensive agriculture, lands that lay over the Alleghenies to the west." Even while Frederick Butler urged his readers to "venerate the plough," farms and farmers continued to migrate west, New England's open fields reverted to forest, and thousands of miles of stone walls, the very symbols of the early settlers' mastery over field and flock, slipped from view.

Ironically, as farms disappeared, flower gardens bloomed. Inspirational writers began to see healthful exercise, for mind and body, in the recreation of floraculture. "The same zeal that fired the formation of benevolent, temperance, anti-slavery, prison reform, and missionary societies," observes Christie H. White in *People and Plants,* "ignited a movement to beautify the home landscape." Charles Hovey, as editor of *The Magazine of Horticulture,* published in Boston, kept track of the movement in his travels to other communities. "In the interior of Massachusetts," he reported in 1839, "the taste of the inhabitants for flower gardens, and particularly for fine ornamental trees, is not surpassed in any part of the Union."

Following the Civil War, the style, purpose, and size of American gardens were influenced by many factors, including the rapid growth of cities and the simultaneous spread of suburbs, the extravagant personal fortunes created by the Industrial Revolution, the emergence of the country's first mass media—magazines—and the advances in plant sciences and technology that helped to propel the United States to the forefront of farm productivity.

"Between 1850 and 1900," Henry Adams once observed, "nearly everyone's existence was exceptional." That would include Liberty Hyde Bailey, a Cornell professor who wrote more than sixty books on gardening and some seven hundred scholarly papers, as well as serving as editor on the influential *Country Life in America,* and Luther Burbank, who introduced over a thousand new plants during a lifetime of improving varieties through his methodical application of Darwin's theories of species variation and selection.

Born and raised on a farm in Lancaster, Massachusetts, Burbank started a truck farm on seventeen acres in nearby Lunenburg in 1869. Certain he could make the farm a success if he could grow better vegetables faster, and inspired by the research and writings of Darwin, he began selecting and saving the seed of his best stock, in hopes of producing superior crops. His first breakthrough was the development of a large, fine-grained, and blight-proof spud that became famous as the Burbank potato and gave rise to the Russet Burbank, which remains the most widely grown potato in the United States.

In 1875, at the age of twenty-six, Burbank left Massachusetts (where the clergy denounced Darwin's theories as the work of the devil) and moved to the horticultural paradise of California. Settling in Santa Rosa, he tinkered with plant strains to develop sweeter plums, everbearing strawberries, thornless roses, spineless cacti (as forage for cattle in deserts), and hundreds of ornamentals, from Abutilon 'Pride of Chile' to several new zinnias. His most famous flower, the Shasta daisy, took "the plant wizard" seventeen years to develop.

In recognition of the need to apply scientific methods to agriculture as the amateur scientist Burbank did, the first Agricultural Experiment Stations were established in California in 1874 and Connecticut in 1875. The nationwide service that eventually formed, tied to land-grant colleges, is still of value both to farmers and home gardeners.

For a time, gardening acquired a social agenda. In 1878, the well-bred ladies of the Massachusetts Horticultural Society organized a "window-gardening" program to keep "children of the laboring classes" out of mischief. In 1887, George Washington Cable founded what became the Northampton (Massachusetts) People's Institution to instill aesthetic values in working people and organized amateur garden competitions in furtherance of that goal. By 1902, public schools in numerous locations were converting playground space to gardens, to teach kids the virtue of hard work.

A burgeoning middle class, under the spell of new large-circulation magazines like *The House Beautiful* and *House and Garden,* turned to gardening to give a personal stamp to suburban manses, and to get their hands dirty in the process. "Whoever would thoroughly enjoy sitting under his vine and under his fig tree should plant them himself," declared Frances Duncan in the April 1912 issue of *The Garden Magazine.* "To buy a place with these already set out is not the same. To hire a man to plant them destroys the peculiar charm."

opposite: Early seed packets are one of the exhibits in the seed museum at Comstock, Ferre & Co., Wethersfield, Connecticut, the oldest continuously operated seed company in the country.

CARROT

PEPPER

BROCCOLI

CHICORY
DA

TO

CELERY

ENDIV

KALE

WATERMELON

Garden styles continued to be influenced by the English example, a romantic ideal first set forth by Victorian poets like Wordsworth and Tennyson, some of whose writings made old-fashioned flowers fashionable, and carried on in more practical ways by eminent garden designers like William Robinson and Gertrude Jekyll. But the United States' centennial celebration in 1876 sparked renewed interest and pride in our Colonial era and led to faithful restorations of Colonial houses and gardens. Meanwhile, American naturists like Henry Thoreau, John Muir, John Burroughs, and Ralph Waldo Emerson, extolling the mystical import of the wild, helped some gardeners to justify their spadework for its spiritual benefits. And by 1904, garden writers, such as the aforementioned George Washington Cable, were calling for the development of an authentic national American garden style, a challenging goal in view of the country's wildly divergent climate conditions.

Without necessarily lifting a spade of their own, many of the mega-millionaires of the late 19th and early 20th centuries contributed greatly to advances in gardening. In 1869, for example, New Bedford, Massachusetts, merchant James Arnold bequeathed $100,000 to launch Harvard's now famous Arnold Arboretum outside of Boston, with its collection of more than seven thousand types of trees and shrubs. Henry F. du Pont drew some of his inspiration for Winterthur from his time spent at the arboretum when he was studying botany and related subjects at Harvard. Whether or not personally interested in gardens, the owners of Newport's famous "cottages," and of the sprawling estate houses that sprung up on Long Island and within range of all the other metropolitan centers of commerce and industry, as well as in the sunny resort climes of Florida and California, invested heavily to make their grounds and gardens worthy of their mansions. So many of them are open to the public today that it would take years for a gardener to visit them all, and untold years more for the gardener to get over the disappointment upon returning home to compare those spectacular landscapes with his or her own garden.

Another source of inspiration for gardeners came with the proliferation of public botanical gardens in the country, beginning in the late 19th and early 20th centuries. "Although based on British precedents," writes Paul Bennett in *The Garden Lover's Guide to the Northeast*, "these gardens are quintessentially American in that they seek to classify, calculate, and inventory nature's bounty in a spirit of eternal curiosity."

The environmental movement, which gained adherents within mainstream America with the publication, in 1962, of *Silent Spring*, Rachel Carson's exposé of DDT, has caused gardeners large and small to reduce or eliminate altogether their reliance on chemicals in their gardens and, perhaps more important, to try to understand the complexities of the natural world, including the kingdom of plants. Taking care of the environment, a multitasking endeavor if ever there was one, is a matter of gardening substance over gardening style. It is about moving forward without abandoning what has come before. Founded in 1975, the Seed Savers Exchange is a kind of Noah's Ark of eighteen thousand varieties of fruit and garden plants, including four thousand types of tomatoes and five hundred apples. Diane and Kent Whealy, the couple who started this immense preservation effort, call their 170-acre domain in Iowa Heritage Farm. In a sense they are looking after the heritage of all gardeners.

opposite: Chinese tree peonies in full bloom at Cricket Hill Garden in Thomaston, Connecticut.

below left: One of the major competitive horticultural classes at the Newport Flower Show every year is "ornamental plants grown in containers," attracting exhibitors in more than fifteen categories. *center:* With its theatrical, stage-set quality, Rosecliff, built in America's Gilded Age, is a dreamy venue for an annual preview party and dinner, held on the front lawn overlooking the Atlantic the night before the flower show opens to the public. *right:* Entrants in the show's artistic classes put the finishing touches on their elaborate floral designs, which fill every room in the "cottage."

EXCURSION: Newport Flower Show

Flower arrangers are like yachtsmen; some prefer competition (yacht races and flower shows), some prefer sailing for its own sake (cruises and home bouquets).

—KATHARINE S. WHITE, *Onward and Upward in the Garden* (1979)

designed by Stanford White and modeled after the Grand Trianon (the garden retreat of Louis XIV at Versailles), was the scene of some of the most extravagant and creative parties of America's Gilded Age—those prosperous decades before a world war, the Depression, and income taxes took their toll.

From Rosecliff's theatrically designed terrace, facing the Atlantic Ocean, its gigantic garden urns overflowing with fuchsia and geraniums, broad marble steps lead down to a flowing lawn. A weathered black-and-white photograph dating from 1910 shows a dozen sleek doyennes of Newport society dressed in costumes evoking "the great women of history." The elegantly robed woman on the top step, holding a torch in her raised left arm, is the spitting image of the Statue of Liberty.

Flash-forward ninety years to watch the women of today's Newport make their way down these same stairs. It is opening night of the Newport Flower Show, and the Preservation Society of Newport County, sponsor of the show, is hosting a cocktail reception for show patrons and other invited guests. The passing parade is a veritable perennial garden of fashion images. Hats with flowers, fresh and fake. Daisies on a pants suit. Red carnations on a chiffon shift. Lavender and peach tulips on a yellow scarf. A mother and daughter in matching outfits showing white and pink hydrangea on a peach background. Cosmos on a long skirt. *Scabiosa* on Capri pants. Peonies on a pair of sandals. A celery green

jacket with Chinese porcelain vases, all filled with flowers, embossed on it.

Most flower shows are held indoors, and even the most high-falutin productions, such as the Chelsea Flower Show in London and the Philadelphia Flower Show, the largest indoor show in the world, cannot escape the pall of their necessarily starkly lit, trade-show-ready settings. The Newport show offers a different experience, especially when, with evening falling, cocktails all around, and the insistent roar of the Atlantic in the background, time itself stands still, and even recedes, as men and women of a certain age appear more youthful and celebratory in the fading light.

Flower shows were first organized in this country by horticultural societies, the oldest being the New York Horticultural Society, founded by prominent botanists, nurserymen, and plantsmen in 1818. By the time of the Civil War, there were more than forty such groups and they all sponsored exhibitions and awarded premiums for prize entries. New varieties of fruits and flowers were introduced at these shows, sometimes with significant effect, as was the case with the Concord grape that made its debut in 1853 and soon became an industry standard.

After the Civil War, women gardeners became increasingly active in horticultural societies, although one authority figure warned them to protect their fragile constitutions by wearing "flannel drawers, India-rubber shoes,

below: The tradition of formal rose gardens at Rosecliff dates from the
mid-1800s, when historian and diplomat George Bancroft built the
original wooden cottage and began to cultivate hybrid tea roses,
picked for their form, size of bloom, color, hardiness, and suitability for
mass bedding, some varieties of which are still on the grounds today.

below left: Classically themed garden urns planted with a variety of specimens provide a colorful counterpoint to the spectacular beauty of Rosecliff's natural setting. *center*: Cut specimens lined up for scrutiny by judges cannot exceed 24 inches in length; horticultural classes include annuals, herbaceous perennials and biennials, flowers or foliage cut from bulbs, rhizomes, or tubers, and woody specimens cut from shrubs or trees. Flower show literature encourages anyone to enter the competition: "Amaze your friends with your green fingers!" *right*: An army of enthusiastic volunteers helps the Preservation Society of Newport County put on the annual event, New England's only outdoor flower show; its purpose is to cultivate awareness of Newport's garden heritage and to raise money for environmentally sound garden and landscape preservation projects in the historic area.

clockwise from top left:
Mrs. Samuel M. V. Hamilton, chairman of the Newport Flower Show committee and avid amateur gardener. Rosecliff's formal architectural styling tends to elicit formal floral compositions from exhibitors, but whimsy is also welcomed by show officials. A spectacular arrangement in shades of green and white graces a planter in one of the cottage's halls. A sumptuous swag of fresh-cut flowers adds a decorative touch to a room heralding Newport's maritime and equestrian traditions.

and a warm shawl" whenever they set forth in their own gardens. Lady gardeners also banded together at the local level in garden clubs, the oldest being the Lexington, Massachusetts, Field and Garden Club, founded in 1876 to maintain the trees lining the streets in that town and in general to promote beautification through new plantings. Today there are thousands of similar garden clubs, as well as societies devoted to individual flower varieties such as orchids or camellias, most of them accepting both male and female members.

These organizations also conduct exhibitions, smaller in scale than the major flower shows but often just as competitive. At the flower show conducted at Rosecliff in 2001, there were horticultural exhibits of ornamental plants grown in containers and of cut specimen flowers, all judged according to prescribed botanical standards, much as pedigree dogs are judged in AKC shows. But the highlight of the show was the flower arrangements in twelve "artistic classes." One class called for arrangements inspired by the floral patterns on Chinese export dinner plates; another, cascading arrangements in tints, tones, and shades of red. Still another class, citing the legendary teamwork of "Bogie and Bacall, Hepburn and Tracy," invited couples to create a design for a summer bouquet, clearly unmindful of the Ogden Nash poem "The Solitude of Mr. Powers," which concludes:

Beware of floral arrangements;
They lead to marital estrangements.

In the classic World War II movie *Mrs. Miniver,* starring Greer Garson and set in a small rural township in England, it will be remembered that the duchess who ran the annual flower show for townspeople, accustomed to walking off with first prize every year, had to bite her stiff upper lip when she was forced to give the top prize to the town stationmaster, for his excellent roses.

The rose gardens at Rosecliff have been cultivated for more than 150 years. During the mid-1800s, the historian and diplomat George Bancroft built the original Rosecliff and planted roses in a five-bed design, cuttings from which were used to develop the hybrid American Beauty, which became the signature rose of the Gilded Age. In 1891, Nevada silver heiress Theresa Fair Oelrichs bought the property, tore down Bancroft's wooden house, and built a palatial mansion.

In 1976, work began on restoring the property's original five-bed design, starting with the garden south of the house, where a statue of Venus stands. The project was undertaken by noted Newport gardener John A. Yule, whose father, Alexander Yule, had been superintendent of Rosecliff for the Oelrichses and its subsequent owners, the Monroes. The beds feature the hybrid tea roses 'Peace', with its classic yellow double flowers, and 'Chicago Peace', a bicolor version. 'Honor' fills the easterly bed, and the climber 'America' is used along the borders.

The garden scheme continues the tradition of cultivating roses established by Rosecliff's first owner—and provides an exemplary venue for a flower show.

1

Inspired Plantsmen

*I am led to reflect how much more
delightful to an undebauched mind is the
task of making improvements on the earth,
than all the vainglory which can be
acquired from ravaging it.*

—GEORGE WASHINGTON, LETTER TO AN ENGLISH FARMER (1790)

T here are gardens of the heart, gardens of the mind, and gardens of the pocketbook, and most of us find something pleasing in all of them. Plantsmen and plantswomen bring those preoccupations together by virtue of their livelihoods. They need to grow that which is both sentimental and sensible in order to stay in business. In their delightful tribute *Legends in the Garden* (2001), Linda Copeland and Allan Armitage single out dozens of plantsmen, both professional and amateur, who discovered cultivars that have become gold-standard offerings in the American plant palette.

The diversity of the gardeners who first recognized the special virtues of certain garden plants is matched by their acuity in observation. These men and women are on a first-name basis with all that grows in and out of their gardens. Like Elizabeth Lawrence, the beloved chronicler of the world of country gardeners who subscribed to southern market bulletins and who, in her own words, "garden for love," such gardeners have a compulsion to put a name on things, especially plants that seem to stand apart from others of their kind.

Thus, Harriet Kirkpatrick, out for a horseback ride in the hills outside Anna, Illinois, in 1910, came upon a hydrangea with a bloom like a snowball, and thought so much of it that she transplanted it into her own garden. Many years later it was finally registered and propagated commercially as *Hydrangea arborescens* 'Annabelle'. Before Allen Lacy became a nationally recognized garden writer, he taught philosophy at a small college in Linwood, New Jersey. He saw an aster in his neighborhood that no one seemed to know anything about, one that grew to four feet tall and produced violet-blue flowers with bright yellow centers. He guessed correctly that it might be a new variety useful to gardeners and subsequently named it after his wife, thus creating *Aster* 'Hella Lacy'. Henry Ross, who singlehandedly created Gardenview Horticultural Park on sixteen acres in Strongsville, Ohio, has introduced dozens of cultivars through his work on the park over the years, from his white-leafed *Ajuga* 'Arctic Fox', to his mildew-resistant *Monarda* 'Gardenview Scarlet' (which he points out is actually a clone, not a cultivar, because it is vegetatively reproduced).

opposite: Roger's Gardens in Corona del Mar, California, can furnish a garden in style. *right:* This New England sculpture garden has been tended by horticulturist Allen Haskell for more than thirty-five years.

"Cultivar names may reflect the person who found or bred the given plant," observes Armitage, a teacher and researcher on new herbaceous crops who directs the University of Georgia Horticulture Gardens, in his introduction to Legends in the Garden; *"however, few people name plants after themselves."*

This brings to mind the greatest plant-namer of all, 18th-century Swedish naturalist Carl Linnaeus, who subdivided the kingdom of plants according to the form and function of the reproductive parts of individual specimens. By this method, which changed the course of science's inquiry into Nature, he arrived at twenty-four classes and numerous orders, genera, and species for further differentiation. When a German botanist named Johann Siegesbeck attacked his sexual system as "loathsome harlotry," Linnaeus saw fit to name after his detractor a particularly obnoxious weed, still known to this day as *Siegesbeckia.*

More typically, however, the plantsman displays an inherent generosity of spirit, and "passes along," as they say in the South, wonderful plants, not weeds, to fellow gardeners. As Elizabeth Lawrence of Charlotte, North Carolina, wrote *The New Yorker* editor Katharine S. White of Maine and Manhattan, early in their twenty-year-long correspondence about plants and people, "I wish you lived next door and I would fill your garden up."

above: One of the largest commercial growers of herb plants on the Eastern Seaboard, Sal Gilbertie still makes room on his farm in Easton, Connecticut, for a vegetable garden and chickens.

Plantsman's World

The most noteworthy thing about gardeners is that they are always optimistic, always enterprising, and never satisfied.

—VITA SACKVILLE-WEST, *Country Notes* (1939)

Like Picasso, legendary plantsman Allen Haskell (who also studied painting, once) doesn't get around much. Instead, the world comes to the artist. In his case, the artist's studio is Haskell's historic home and garden center, a patch of Eden surviving amid the shopping-mall sprawl of New Bedford, Massachusetts. This is where the Pope got a pair of rose standards for the Vatican. This is where Jackie O. got her favorite flowers, cosmos and daisies, to decorate the church for her daughter's, Caroline Kennedy's, wedding. This is where the proprietor offhandedly pronounces, "If you ever have a problem with a flower arrangement, put blue in it."

So, leave the highway behind, take a right on Shawmut Avenue, and turn at the sign of the peacock, announcing "ALLEN P. HASKELL, PLANTS & COMPLIMENTS" (*sic*). Enter a world of botanical wonders, for the term *garden center* is hardly adequate to describe the crazy-quilt of beautiful gardens here. Repeat visits are obligatory, because change is always in the air. Haskell thinks nothing of uprooting plants, even mature trees, and moving them from one end of the property to the other, for improved aesthetic effect. As one admirer, the artist and garden writer Abbie Zabar, has observed, "Nothing can stop Allen Haskell from doing it again if he can do it better." Every fall he plants ten thousand bulbs of green tulips. After they have bloomed in the spring,

opposite: One of the largest producers of topiaries in the United States, Allen Haskell's nursery trains young myrtle, ivy, rosemary, bay laurel, lavender, and santolina to grow into standards and as spheres, "lollipop heads," and other beguiling shapes.

above: Dwarf Alberta spruce trained into three-tiered topiaries stand like a row of ancient Chinese warriors in Allen Haskell's nursery in New Bedford, Massachusetts.

loath to look at their expiring foliage, he digs them all up and gives them away to his favorite customers.

Some seventy-five rare camellias, from peppermint pink to deeper hues, are sprinkled throughout the display gardens. Near one of Allen's classic Lord & Burnham greenhouses stands a huge and gorgeous flowering dogwood, *Cornus florida,* a specimen more than 250 years of age that, Haskell believes, may well be the oldest of its kind in the United States. Next to it stands another rarity: the Chinese dove tree, *Davidia involucrata,* which he started from a cutting taken from a tree in Harvard's Arnold Arboretum two decades ago. Also known as the handkerchief tree or ghost tree, it bloomed for the first time one

recent spring, cause for joyous celebration among the family and friends who make up Haskell's loyal staff. Son David, a talented landscape designer in his own right; Allen's daughter, Felecia; and wife, Ellena, all work in the garden center, as does Briton John Mitchell, the head propagator, and Gene Bertrand, Allen's longtime companion, also an accomplished grower.

In the gardening world, Haskell is an American original, seamlessly juggling his deep-seated Puritan work ethic with an appreciative taste for Dewar's, chilled, no ice, at his daily lunch stop, Rosies, up the road from the nursery, and shamelessly balancing contradictory opinions, about color, say. One minute he will tell you, "Every color has its place in the garden. Don't be prejudiced . . . just find the right place for it." The next (on a drive through town), he'll remark, "Godawful magenta azaleas grouped around a chartreuse Japanese maple! What insipid nerds dreamt up that combination?" At the same time, he admits, "I'm known to knock on the doors of strangers to tell them how good their garden looks."

When Richard Churchill, himself a horticulturist, was assigned to write a magazine story about Haskell, he gingerly made inquiries about the man, and heard

him described, variously, as "revered, eccentric, New England's horticultural legend, outrageous, a mentor to many, an artist, a visionary, a perfectionist, kind-hearted, savage, able to paint with plants, a plant promoter, a trend setter, a cutting-edge horticulturalist . . . and a man who suffers no fools."

Actually, Haskell says he has thrown out only two customers in fifty years, most recently a man who insisted on standing in a bed of his green tulips. Allen has a wicked sense of humor, which he says he inherited from his father. His parents

made a fateful decision in his behalf when he was two and diagnosed with brain cancer. They were told that by removing the tumor through an eye socket, sacrificing one eye, the boy's chances of survival would be better, and that was the course chosen. The surgery was successful. About convalescing in his backyard, Haskell recalls, "I got to know every bug and living thing." A star plantsman was born. "I'm in love with horticulture," he says today. "I sleep it, eat it, drink it, live it."

left and above: A lifetime of planning by master grower Allen Haskell has resulted in a garden center with the attributes of a world-class botanical garden. Mixing annuals and perennials in unusual combinations of color and form, Haskell creates planters that provide summer-long beauty and charm.

Allen, well-versed in the psychology of the average gardener, points to a favorite bit of doggerel posted on the wall in his office:

Oh Lord of little things,
Reward all my labors
And make my garden
A little bit better than my neighbor's.

Haskell is as famous for his plants as his personality, for example his collection of azaleas, many of them more than fifty years old, and none of them magenta. He is famous for his collection of hosta, a jumbo version of which he recently hybridized and named 'David Allen Haskell', after his son. All proceeds from the sale of the Haskell hosta go into a scholarship fund for a grandson. (A Boston-area garden of his design contains more than six hundred hosta plants from his nursery.) He is famous for his "impeccable topiary designs," as friend and fan Martha Stewart has described them, "that

reveal the beauty of the plants' textures, shapes, and forms." He produces thirty thousand topiaries a year, among them elegant spheres of ivy, bay laurel and rosemary, three-tiered myrtle with pineapple-shaped tops, lollipop heads of lavender, westringia and santolina, and stately scented geraniums. "His creativity with plants," declares Martha, "is unrivaled in the world of horticulture."

Haskell loves animals almost as much as he loves plants. Golden pheasants, peacocks, and fancy fowl strut within their handsomely crafted pens at the north end of the garden center, an unexpected delight for first-time visitors. The birds are housed a few steps from Haskell's own Federal-style home, originally part of a farmstead dating from 1725, listed on the Massachu-

opposite: One of Haskell's fourteen greenhouses. *left:* A jumbo hosta cultivar, named for Haskell's son. *below:* One of many colorful fowl on exhibit. *bottom:* The sign at the entrance. *overleaf:* The plantsman's house is the oldest residence in New Bedford, dating from a 1725 farmstead.

tams for her very own.) Haskell's fondness for exotic animals extends even to his camel, Lester, whose notoriously bad breath apparently hindered efforts to breed him. When Allen finally located a compatible mate, he named her Listerine.

Since 1949 Haskell has served the New England Flower Show, the world's third-largest indoor horticultural exhibition, in many capacities, from judge to exhibitor. (When he has had a falling out with the powers that be at the Boston show, he has retaliated by exhibiting at the Providence show.) He has been honored by the Amer-

above and right: In the living room, an extensive library of garden books is joined by the friendly company of mid-19th-century ceramic jars in the image of roosters and hens, originally used to store hard-boiled eggs and later brought into service as rustic serving dishes.

setts Registry of Historic Houses. Haskell keeps numerous other animals, including heritage breeds of livestock, on a fifty-five-acre farm he owns in nearby Fairhaven. (Once, when the aforementioned Martha paid a visit and saw his collection of English game bantams, she expressed such admiration that he gave her a male and two female white-crested black Polish ban-

ican Horticultural Society as Nurseryman of the Year, but a hometown tribute means more to him: the George C. Perkins Presi-

above: The Haskell home is furnished with New England antiques, including a gateleg dining room table dating from 1610. Allen obtained the hand-carved marble figure propped between the windows, originally part of a water fountain, from a customer for 50 dollars' worth of pachysandra. *above right:* Botanical images in the upstairs hallway include four small prints from the late 18th to early 19th century and two larger prints depicting *Mesembryanthemum glabrum* and *Nymphaea stellata.* *right:* The eclectic mind of Allen Haskell is reflected in the contents of his desk: peacock feathers, images of domestic animals, a Mardi Gras mask, and a rare copy of *Flora of New Bedford and Shores of Buzzards Bay,* by E. Williams Hervey, published in 1911.

above: In a half-forgotten corner of one of Allen Haskell's many work areas, pots, watering cans, and old signs gather dust. *opposite:* By contrast, a greenhouse filled with healthy-looking topiaries is ready to open its doors to the public as the last threat of a killing frost fades in the New England spring. *right:* A bulletin board on a wall in the nursery office is covered with prize ribbons, judge's badges, news clippings from the world of horticulture, and handwritten notes from satisfied customers.

dent's Award, given by the Waterfront Historic Area League (WHALE), in 2001. That citation reads:

His extraordinary career in horticulture has made him an American treasure. His commitment to the preservation of his home and gardens has made him a New Bedford treasure. His untiring effort to provide beauty and style to so many in our community has made him a friend.

Haskell works tirelessly, morning to night, day after day, to keep his gardens fresh, his greenhouse full, and his plant materials enticing to the most discriminating of gardeners. It's hardly the most lucrative calling: "We're like a benevolent society, no one really makes any money." Yet it is deeply rewarding in many ways.

A back room at Haskell's nursery is plastered with horticulture awards, the first of which he won at age nineteen with, as he recalls, an all-green garden. But he places precious little stock in such forms of recognition, being much more interested in his next hands-on chore in the greenhouse or garden. "Gardening is today," he says; "forget last week and next week."

And forget all those silver bowls, too, the ones that accompanied the numerous awards he has received in the course of a half-century of masterful garden-design work. Allen Haskell sold the silver long ago—to pay for his son's education in the field of horticulture.

Rose Story Farm

I have read a bit about the history of roses, and I am convinced there is a film in it.

—BARBARA DAMROSCH, *The Garden Primer* (1988)

opposite: The climbing rose 'Altissimo' produces large, single-petaled red blooms from April through December on the grounds of Rose Story Farm.

It is Saturday morning and Danielle and Dr. William Hahn are leading a small group of rose fanciers on a tour of Rose Story Farm, a 15-acre paradise of roses—some 15,000 bushes representing 119 varieties and counting—in Southern California's fertile Carpinteria Valley. Danielle, formerly proprietor of a successful gift and children's clothing shop in nearby Santa Barbara, and Bill, a gastroenterologist at the Sansum–Santa Barbara Medical Foundation Clinic, share a love and knowledge of roses that casually surfaces throughout the tour.

"This is Pat Austin from the English hybridizer David Austin," says Danielle, stopping at a bush filled with coral blooms and snipping a sample. "It's a one-of-a-kind color for a rose, with a gold reverse, and it still looks pretty after its petals start to drop because the stamens are so pretty." Proffering the cutting to a visitor, she says, "Put your face into the flower and inhale for four or five seconds. Almost all our roses have fragrance. They are mostly a combination of old roses, European varieties, and pre-1950 American hybrid teas, with unusual shapes and colors and scents that commercial growers have bred out for the sake of certain shapes and forms and for longer life as a cut flower."

To the Hahns, the industry standard single-stem cut rose with little or no

Inspired Plantsmen, Passionate Collectors, and Singular Visions in the World of Gardening

above: Climbing 'Cecile Brunner' roses envelop Hydrangea Cottage in color, while flowering lavender fills the front garden and 'Sally Holmes', a single-petaled hybrid musk, and the climbing tea rose 'Sombreuil' are in bloom along the path leading to the guest cottage.

fragrance is anathema. Rather than trim to get a single long-stemmed blossom as most rose growers do, they let the side buds develop and cut the whole spray—some with up to ten blossoms—to use in bouquets. The more than ten thousand roses sent out weekly from Rose Story Farm are imbued with pale, romantic hues and deep fragrances. Danielle divides the aromas of roses into four categories for her visitors.

"First and foremost are the florals—the roses that smell of rose, violet, or lily," she says. "Then there are the fruit-scented roses, smelling of berry, apple, lemon, or melon. Still others have a spicy scent, whether it's clove, licorice, pepper, or myrrh. And still others are sweet with the

hint of honey or vanilla." (One of the few nonfragrant roses she grows is 'Fame', "an American hybrid tea rose with a gorgeous raspberry color, moderately disease-resistant and prolific—with a vase life of up to two weeks, compared with an average duration for roses in water of four or five days.")

A mixed flock of geese and ducks, as if in imitation of the tour group, waddles across the lawn embracing a compound of cottages on the property, prompting Bill to point out, "One duck per acre takes care of our snail problem." The roses are fertilized with compost and other organic materials. Three pointers, including the family pet, Patch, keep raccoons, coyotes, and mountain lions thinking twice about descending onto the farm from the surrounding wild.

"This is a new climbing rose called 'Berries and Cream'," Danielle says at a later stage on the tour. "We sent three thousand six-foot stems of this variety to the MGM Grand in Las Vegas last week."

The Hahn farm supplies roses to individuals as well as to wholesalers and the boutique florists and designers who cater to celebrities and socialites. "Maybe only someone like you could understand my love of the rose and how special it made my wedding," one satisfied Ohio bride e-mailed Danielle following her wedding.

"About one hour before I had to leave for the church," she related, "my sister was impatiently waiting for me to finish arranging flowers and she asked, 'Do you care more about your hair, makeup, and nails, or your flowers?' Without hesitation, I had to respond, 'The flowers!'"

Dani, as friends call her, will also supply rose petals in volume to clients for strewing at weddings or turning into glamorous centerpieces. Two hundred roses yield about six gallons of petals, she says. When roses are cut intact for shipping, they are cleaned and dethorned by hand,

below left: Danielle Hahn and her mother, Patti Dall'Armi, prepare flowers for shipment in the rose prep room. The bulletin board features three blue ribbons Dani won in her first rose show. *below:* The rose 'Fame', "an American hybrid tea rose with a gorgeous raspberry color," Dani says, is in a pot next to freshly harvested lemons.

overleaf: Visiting floral designer Beth Goodman and her dog Clover set forth to gather blooms. The center of operations at Rose Story Farm was originally a stable.

using heavy gloves, instead of a machine or a tool. Bunches are then banded in raffia and wrapped in waxed butcher paper. The elegantly packaged roses of Rose Story Farm go wherever Federal Express has the capability of delivering them.

top right: A mixed bouquet of garden roses.
above: The Hahns, with the help of the family pointer, harvest sprays of the rose 'Celebrity'.

Still later on the tour, Bill relates that the couple's present acreage has been under cultivation since the 1880s, when a Boston family planted 634 acres in walnuts. A lemon orchard succeeded walnuts in the 1920s and lemons in turn gave way to avocados in the 1970s. Since that time com-

mercial nurseries, specializing in field-grown flowers, have dominated the landscape in Carpinteria. More recently, an influx of ambitious growers primarily from Holland has transformed the open fields into a sea of greenhouses, enabling year-round, twenty-four-hours-a-day growing

clockwise from left: 'Paul Bocuse', a shrub rose developed by the French hybridizer Jean Pierre Guillot, is part of a lush bouquet with white hydrangea and purple amaranthus. The cooler came from the old Miramar Hotel in Santa Barbara and is used to chill and display arrangements; sprays of the rose 'Eden' are drying on top. Beth Goodman puts together a flower arrangement for a wedding.

As the tour continues, Danielle speaks of her favorite modern rose hybridizers: David Austin of England; Jean Pierre Guillot of France; and, with warmth, a recently deceased fellow Californian, Oliver Weeks. "Ollie was really the premier American hybridizer," she notes, "developing some fifty roses over a forty-year career." Since 1988, Tom Carruth has succeeded Weeks in developing successful new rose hybrids,

conditions and a hundredfold increase in production. Rose Story Farm, however, harks back to the earlier agrarian traditions of Carpinteria—a small family operation emphasizing quality over quantity.

"Most evenings, while other couples sip cocktails or relax in hot tubs," says a friend, "the Hahns find their best moments outside, working the rows." Sometimes they are accompanied by their sons, Will and Geoffrey, and by Dani's parents, Patti and Lorenzo Dall'Armi, who drive over from Montecito, "to snip off spent blooms, shape the bushes and pull up weeds, all the while chatting about family affairs and the day's events."

above: Saturday-morning tours expose visitors to the mystique and the methodology of growing old garden roses. *right:* 'Celebrity', a yellow rose developed by California hybridizer Oliver Weeks. *opposite:* The former horse barn, now covered with the sweetly perfumed climber 'Cécile Brünner'.

which routinely take eight to ten years to be properly evaluated in field trials; one of his recent introductions is the chamois-colored 'Marilyn Monroe', which Dani predicts "will be in everybody's rose garden one day."

below: A hillside is planted with 'Scenti-mental', a red-striped floribunda, the orange 'Mojave', a 1950s hybrid tea, and the lavender 'Heirloom', another hybrid tea.

The visitors come to the base of a hill planted with roses. A venerable avocado tree stands alone on the brow of the hill, outlined against the sky. The Santa Barbara hills loom in the background. The area's climate, tempered by mountain and sea, allows Dani's roses to repeat bloom six or more times a year.

"The soil on the hillside is shallow and quite rocky," Danielle points out. "Yet the roses flourish there, because air circulation is better on the hill. The roses at the base of the hill, with less air circulation, have more problems with rust and mildew." Pausing, she adds, "We've left a lot of our mistakes in the ground, but that's okay. Once you accept such things, it's easier to be a gardener."

The Hahns bought the property in 1990, moving from nearby Montecito. At the time the land was run-down and neglected, but it came with a three-story Victorian farmhouse, a cluster of century-old cottages—themselves neglected and uninhabitable at the time—and a thick-walled horse barn.

"At the time I was not planning to get into the commercial growing of roses," Danielle tells the group as they move away from the hill. "But both Bill and I had rose lovers in our family tree—each of our grandmothers was an ardent rosarian—and I immediately planted about four hundred rosebushes just for ourselves."

The decision to start a business came when the family realized the horses Bill

kept on a few acres had to go. The turning point occurred when one of the Hahns' sons and a friend were pitched off the horses they were riding. The boys were uninjured, but five days later Bill got rid of the horses and set to work transforming the horse corral into a new field for antique roses. To make room for two more fields, he pulled out hundreds of past-their-prime lemon trees with a bulldozer.

In preparation for her first year in business, Danielle pored over hundreds of rose books and catalogs, "like a kid in a candy store," to select a thousand rosebushes. The selection process continues today albeit on a smaller scale, as she strives to diversify her collection "of varieties you never see outside of private gardens," to serve an ever-increasing customer base of discriminating rose lovers.

These roses include the whites and pastels most popular with brides; the lavenders, purples, and salmons that go so well with interior decors; the novelty roses, "with color stripes and tips that are fun to grow, and are like an exclamation point in the garden"; and the classic colors of red, pink, and yellow.

"We're putting classic red roses back on the map," she says as she brings the tour to a conclusion in front of a planting of Isabel

Renaissance, one of fourteen varieties of red roses grown at Rose Story Farm. Isabel is not all romance, however. "The very tall shoots make Isabel difficult to prune," Dani laughs. "When we come out to work in this patch, we call it 'going into the tiger cage.'"

At that moment Patch, the stoic-faced family pointer, bounds onto the scene, and Danielle Hahn obliges him with a pat. "And now," she says, turning to the visitors, most of whom by this time are each holding one or two blooms cupped in their hands, like earnest supplicants to the glory of the rose itself, "let's have our picnic lunch. Patch and I will lead the way."

top: An array of mixed bouquets. *above:* Angel, one of the Hahns' many cats, with their dog Patch and a gathering basket of freshly cut 'Celebrity' roses.

La Casa Pacifica

To sum up enormous wisdom for you in a sentence, the formula is simple: grow the most beautiful flowers you have ever seen or heard of, going through the year.

—HENRY MITCHELL, *One Man's Garden* (1992)

Gavin Herbert was in junior high school when he had one of his first entrepreneurial brainstorms. The family home in the San Fernando Valley came with a substantial apricot orchard that at the time was heavy with fruit, with no one to harvest it. With World War II under way, strict rationing was in force, and large numbers of American families were canning and preserving fruits and vegetables to extend the growing season.

Gavin placed a small ad in the *Los Angeles Times* inviting people to come down on the weekend and pick ripe apricots for the bargain price of one dollar a crate. The only problem was, he had not told his parents about the plan, and they happened to be hosting a party for their friends that weekend. No problem: The pickers went in one gate and the invited guests went in the other. And at the end of the day, twelve-year-old Gavin had three or four hundred dollars in his pocket.

Decades later, Gavin Herbert is still a consummate grower of businesses, and of gardens. In fact, he and his wife, Ninetta, live in one of the most beautiful garden spots in all of California, a traditional Spanish-style courtyard residence overlooking

opposite: A bignonia, or cross vine, with its trumpet-shaped flowers, frames a side entrance to the plant-filled courtyard of Ninetta and Gavin Herbert's Spanish-style residence in southern California.

above: La Casa Pacifica
made history in 1973
when, functioning as
the Western White
House, it provided the
venue for the signing of
the Salt II Treaty by
President Richard Nixon
and Soviet Communist
Party General Secretary
Leonid Brezhnev.

the grounds of the Chelsea Flower Show in London, where it had won the Best in Show award. The Herberts go to the Chelsea show almost every year in search of new ideas for their own gardens, and for Roger's Gardens, the family-owned garden center in nearby Corona del Mar that is itself a magnet for gardeners. Known in the area as "the Disneyland of garden centers," according to Lew Whitney, who directs horticultural operations there, its carefully planned display gardens offer customers a host of planting ideas. The Herberts' facility is also famous for its lushly planted hanging baskets and for its selection of statuary and garden ornaments of all kinds, "and I'm one of our best customers," quips Ninetta.

As for La Casa, "initially I wanted to try to re-create what the gardens might have been like at their peak when the original owners lived here," says Gavin Herbert. Hamilton H. Cotton, a prosperous real estate and cotton broker from Chicago, and his wife, Victoria, an heir to the gigantic Dominguez Ranch that once contained all of present-day Los Angeles

the Pacific Ocean (and some of the best surfing waters on the West Coast) in San Clemente. La Casa Pacifica is surrounded by gardens that the Herberts, with help from their longtime associate, Lew Whitney, have thoughtfully installed over the past two decades, including a brick-walled double-axis garden imported directly from

County, had built the house in 1926 as part of a 5,000-acre estate that included a horse farm and a racetrack. Among the cherished plantings that survive from that era are towering palms and Monterey cypress, interspersed throughout the property. "But really, when they lived here it was more of a desert climate, without irrigation. They were essentially limited to creating a Mediterranean garden. We have much more scope."

In fact, the six-acre estate contains subtly diverse microclimates that permit a variety of specimens to grow today, including plants not commonly successful

left and below: Masses of petunias thrive in the heat and add interest to steps leading to a pool house. After the Herberts acquired the property from the Nixons, they built the pool house (designed by Gavin Herbert's childhood friend Diane Johnson). The couple's most cherished plantings include the towering palms and Monterey cypresses that date from the era when the land was first settled. *overleaf:* The statuary and furniture that lend character to the estate are the special province of Ninetta Herbert.

left: Geometrically shaped gardens on the northwest side of the house, framed in boxwood, are planted with seasonal flowers, such as impatiens in midsummer, to provide year-long color. The 30-foot-tall magnolia was started from a cutting First Lady Pat Nixon took from a tree Andrew Jackson had planted at the White House in the early 19th century. *below left:* All the hard components of the English wall garden at La Casa Pacifica, including a large quantity of 200-year-old bricks, are from a garden once judged Best in Show at London's Chelsea Flower Show. They were acquired by the Herberts in the course of a shopping expedition for Roger's Gardens, then later reassembled on the grounds at their house. *below:* Meandering trails take visitors from garden to garden, vista to vista. Decomposed granite excavated on the property was used to make the paths.

in Southern California, such as Siberian iris, 'Iceberg' roses, and clematis vines. The shady and wind-buffeted oceanfront terrain gives way to a sunny interior patio filled with olive trees, then to the tropically inclined area by the swimming pool and pavilion, where bougainvillea and lemon trees thrive, amid masses of potted flowering plants, while other protected inland sites are home to a profusion of rose, vegetable, herb, and flower gardens. A cottage garden on the northeast side of the house, visible from the dining room, is filled with mostly white flowers, including Shasta daisies, delphiniums, marguerites, and foxglove.

"The vegetable garden is one of my favorite places nowadays," says Ninetta, "because that's where the grandsons, ages four and five, like to play, especially with the flock of chickens we have. Collecting eggs, pulling carrots, and eating them— these are all the activities that I think will give them warm and lasting memories." Having grown up in Indiana, Ninetta remembers the enthusiasm with which her grandmother gardened. "I would fashion dolls from the flowers of her hollyhocks," she recalls. "But I hated her peonies because they had ants on them. Little did I know that the ants helped in pollinating the flowers. Anyway, now peonies are one of my favorite flowers, even though they are one of the few plants we just can't grow here because of our mild winters."

La Casa's first owners, the Cottons, were prominent figures in the Democratic party, chauffeuring their influential friends down the coast on weekends by private railway car. During the 1930s, President Franklin D. Roosevelt used to play poker with Cotton and other party cronies in a gazebo on the estate. A gigantic elephant topiary of fern pine *(Podocarpus gracilior)* now on the property signifies the change in ownership and political affiliation that occurred in 1969. President and Mrs. Richard M. Nixon moved in and turned the place into their Western White House. Bulletproof glass went up around the pool. Perimeter plantings were allowed to grow

above: At ocean's edge, a mature grove of Monterey cypress trees, planted when the house was first built in the 1920s, provides an ecosystem different from anywhere else on the property.

above: The arched windows and doors of the living room provide generous prospects of the gardens and, in the distance, the cypress grove overlooking the Pacific. The painting over the china cabinet by an early California artist is one of several examples of regional art collected by the Herberts.

into great thickets as visual protection.

"It was like a jungle," recalls Gavin, who became chief of the volunteer brigade from Roger's Gardens that provided garden maintenance for the Nixons on weekends during their residency. "You couldn't even see the ocean from the house."

Gavin had been friends with Nixon advisor Bob Haldeman since their college days and he had co-served as financial chairman of the 1972 presidential campaign. His friendship with the First Family deepened during his tenure as "head gardener." Pat Nixon "liked her gardens wild and natural," he recalls, "nothing too fancy." Once, she took a cutting from a magnolia tree that Andrew Jackson had planted at the White House in the early

19th century and successfully transplanted it to the Western White House. Now grown to 30 feet, it has become the focal point of the garden on the northwest side of the house. Today, Pat's garden gloves, worn to a frazzle, are on exhibit in the Nixon Presidential Library in Yorba Linda, California. (Gavin Herbert serves on the library's board of directors.)

The frequent visits of heads of state and other dignitaries brought international renown to La Casa Pacifica. "Leonid Brezhnev expressed an interest in seeing the place when he was with President Nixon at Camp David in 1973," Gavin recalls. "We had three days' notice to get the place spruced up." While they were here, Brezhnev and Nixon signed the his-

toric Salt II Treaty to limit the threat of nuclear war, an event captured in one of many photographs from the era on one wall in the pavilion house. After resigning from office, however, Nixon experienced a period of brooding isolation that beautiful gardens and a beautiful ocean view could not allay. Gavin Herbert, who had traveled to China with Nixon, actually met him in the house "on the sad day of his return," and continued as his friend. "We gradually got him to the point where he'd meet with outside groups, and as he regained his strength he developed a positive approach to his life once again." After the former president decided to move to the East Coast, Gavin helped to facilitate that transition by agreeing to buy the property. As it

above left: The cottage garden visible from the dining room is filled with mostly white flowers, including Shasta daisies, delphiniums, marguerites, and foxglove.
above: A statue of Ceres, the goddess of the harvest, greets visitors in the entry hall; Ninetta Herbert found the figure at Roger's Gardens.
left: The sitting room adjacent to the master bedroom is a favorite location for reading or taking in the views.

turned out, Nixon did indeed rehabilitate his image in his final years, especially as an expert on foreign policy—through books, speeches, and media interviews.

Meanwhile, Gavin Herbert had grown Allergan, a company he started with his father in 1950, into a billion-dollar global health care company providing eye care and specialty pharmaceutical products worldwide, with headquarters in Irvine, California, and branches in Ireland, Brazil, and Europe. A pharmacist himself, Gavin Senior had owned a number of apothecary shops in Los Angeles before launching Allergan to market new eye care products for people suffering from allergies, starting with the first eye drops to contain antihistamines. (Botox is the firm's latest cutting-

edge product.) The younger Herbert served as the firm's CEO from 1961 to 1991 and its chairman from 1977 to 1995.

In honor of the family's apothecary heritage, a collection of ceramic vessels used by pharmacists from as early as the 15th century, some of which came from the shops belonging to Gavin's father, makes a striking display inside La Casa Pacifica. Appropriately, for a household enthralled by the beauty of flowers, many of the vessels are illustrated with vivid images of the botanical specimens that have formed the basis for so many healing agents of the past.

In the Kingdom of Herbs

Lovely and timeless, rooted at once in gardens and in life, the great herbs come to the gardener's hand our most noble heritage of green.

—HENRY BESTON, *Herbs and the Earth* (1935)

The raised-bed stock gardens, fecund growing fields, and state-of-the-art greenhouses of Sal Gilbertie in Easton, Connecticut, are the product of more than a half-century of hands-on cultivation of hundreds of varieties of herbal plants, from aloe vera to Roman wormwood, most of which find their way every spring and summer from the Gilbertie wholesale complex to garden centers and nurseries along the eastern seaboard from Maine to Virginia.

"We believe we grow the healthiest and highest quality herb plants you can buy," says Sal, the third-generation owner of the business, who points to the rich, fungus-free soil base in which he grows the herbs as a secret of his success. "We mix our own soil from an organic compost base which we sterilize through the use of steam heat. To this we add fibrous peat and long-needle yellow pine bark, a natural fungus retardant. Then we blend in organic fertilizers," adding, "we learned long ago that most gardeners are reluctant to grow plants, especially those destined to flavor the foods we eat, with the help of anything chemical. If you use proper gardening techniques, there is no reason you can't garden organically and successfully."

opposite: A variegated-leaf sage is one of more than 400 herb varieties that Sal Gilbertie grows on his farm in Easton, Connecticut.

top: On his way to make a delivery in his vintage pickup truck, Sal Gilbertie exhibits the buoyant personality that informs his style as a popular author and lecturer on herb plants. *above:* A selection of freshly harvested culinary herbs.

leafed parsley; baked calamari seasoned with lemon verbena and dill; and broiled salmon in lemony dill and fennel sauce.

"Harvesting herbs from garden and farm is a delight throughout the growing season," Sal observes. "Putting them to use in the home in so many beautiful and savory ways at Christmas, when here in Connecticut all growth in the plant kingdom has come to a halt, is a deeply satisfying pleasure."

Gilbertie brings herbs into his own home as a matter of course, and never more prominently than on Christmas Eve every year, when he and his wife, Marie, play host to dozens in the Gilbertie clan. The table is set for a banquet, its centerpiece a wreath of cedar, boxwood, and holly, with white candles, white roses, white daisies, and eucalyptus. At the place settings for all the women guests, Sal sets out a red rose with three or four sprigs of herbs. "When we all sit down, I take a moment to remind everyone of the symbolic associations of the herbs—thyme for courage, sage for longevity, rosemary for remembrance, and parsley for festivity," he says, "just to sound a brief serious note before our celebration begins."

The Christmas Eve dinner itself is a fish-lover's feast in the Italian tradition, with seven varieties of fresh seafood prepared according to savory, old family recipes, including shrimp sautéed in oil with garlic, red pepper, and handfuls of fresh minced savory, oregano, and flat-

The author of three garden books and a frequent lecturer on gardening, Gilbertie is a proselytizer on the beneficial aspects of gardening as well as a round-the-clock farmer and businessman.

"Gardening is like a devotional activity for mind and body," he says. "It brings people in touch with the realities of land and sky, heat and cold, rain, wind and drought, and the life cycle itself." His enthusiasm for his subject is infectious. Every spring he conducts free workshops on "maximum-production vegetable gardening" at his retail garden center in nearby Westport.

"How many ripe tomatoes should you get off a single tomato plant?" he will ask his audience, seated comfortably in the middle of the demonstration gardens he has designed and built over the years.

below: After taking cuttings of thyme, workers will plant the sprigs to develop them as new plants. *right:* All plants in Sal Gilbertie's greenhouses bear informative labeling. *bottom:* The bucolic setting of Gilberties Herb Gardens in Easton, Connecticut.

"Fifty?" someone calls out, adding, "but I know that's high."

"High?" Sal will retort. "As a matter of fact that's low." And then he'll tell them, "One year I made a point to keep track of how much fruit I got off one of our plants. I harvested a hundred and fifty-eight good-sized tomatoes. And that doesn't count a dozen green tomatoes I grabbed off the same plant before the first killing frost in the fall!"

And now that Sal has his audience salivating about the abundance of vine-ripened tomatoes in their future, he proceeds to share all his secrets. Raise your beds. Plant in straight rows. Avoid overcrowding. Use onions as your perimeter guards against pests. Fertilize with rabbit manure if you can find it. . . . On and on for an hour, until the attendees, their notebooks ripe with ideas for obtaining 25 to

30 green bell peppers from a single plant, 50 cukes from a cucumber vine trained to a fence, and 265 string beans from a pole bean variety growing on a trellis, are ready to go home and start digging.

The Gilbertie family business dates back to 1922, when Sal's grandfather began growing cut flowers commercially both in fields and in greenhouses in several locations in southeastern Connecticut. That business grew and prospered until the advent of air freight after World War II. With Florida growers able to ship cut flowers in volume, cut-flower growers in the Northeast could not compete. Sal's father, who by now had joined the business, was forced to diversify.

"My father's specialties were asters, snapdragons, chrysanthemums, zinnias, and vegetables," Sal says. "He had never grown herbs commercially, though he knew how, having always included a number of them in our kitchen garden and mixed in with our perennial flowers. He used some herbs as companion plants—to help keep pests away from certain vegetables—but mainly he grew them for our kitchen."

Shifting production into herb plants on a large scale, Sal recalls, began by chance. One of their wealthy customers, a woman known as the countess (who had made a fortune in the perfume business, and who always tipped the boys who delivered pails of flowers for her from the nursery with a sampling of her product), called one fall day in 1958 to announce plans for a huge formal herb garden, to be pie-shaped with twelve slices, each with sixty plants of a different variety.

"My father did not want to disappoint the countess," Sal relates, "so that winter in the greenhouses, he sowed not sixty but one hundred herb plants in each of the twelve categories—to be sure he ended up with all he needed to fill her order. The plantings were particularly successful, so in the spring, when the herbs were ready for moving outdoors, he found himself with quite a surplus.

"We delivered the big order to the countess," Sal continues, "picked up our perfume, and came back to the garden center. Then we put the extra herb seedlings, which had been moved into four-inch pots, out with the rest of our plants for sale. When they sold out—almost immediately—my father turned to me and said, 'Sal, quick, learn about herbs.'"

And so began an odyssey through the kingdom of herbs that continues to this day.

opposite: The stock gardens from which Sal Gilbertie propagates herbs are planted in raised beds, increasing the depth of the soil base and improving drainage. *top:* A window box of herbs adds a decorative touch to the chicken coop. *above:* When in flower, herbs rival other plants in beauty if not in size.

below and opposite: The Santa Barbara Farmer's Market, open year-round, rain or shine, brings together the best small farmers in the area and the most discriminating food and flower shoppers. With more than 320 such markets across the state, California leads all states in the growing movement known variously as "organic farming," "family farming," "community supported agriculture," "slow food," or just plain "good food." Visitors may stop by the market, at the corner of Santa Barbara and Cota Streets, with a short list in hand, but most go home with all they can carry.

EXCURSION: Southern California

It is almost an ever-abiding joy of our Southern California life that we may be out of doors.

—HAZEL WOODS WATERMAN, *On My Friend's Porch* (1902)

CALIFORNIA IS GARDENING WRIT LARGE—ENDLESS SEAS OF GREEN IN

bounteous Imperial Valley, the world-class vineyards of Napa and Sonoma Valleys, the plethora of skilled, creative seedsmen, plantsmen, and growers of every stripe toiling in their gardens and fields, in the tradition of Luther Burbank, up and down the state. Not to mention the fabulous estate gardens, from Villa Narcissa in Rancho Palos Verdes to the Huntington Botanical Gardens in San Marino, all of them the products of unimaginable personal wealth, perfectionist desire, horticultural adventurism, and a benign sun.

In all the world, only the Mediterranean, South Africa, and Australia are blessed with as mild and salubrious a climate for growing so many different plant forms, and over such a long, productive growing season. Even a random swing on less-traveled roads through portions of one southerly wedge of California gives a glimpse into the rich and ever-changing growing traditions of a region unlike any other in America.

The movable feast that is the Santa Barbara Certified Farmers Market exemplifies a newly popular movement that is putting food consumers face to face with the fresh fare of small farmers, with smiles on both sides. A year-round purveyor of just-picked fruits, vegetables, herbs, and flowers that rotates through six locations in the Santa Barbara area, this market is a treat for the senses, and, some would say, the conscience.

"People want a piece of fruit or an ear of corn that wasn't picked in Mexico and shipped for two thousand miles," declares one such farmer. Although farm markets account for a very small fraction of total farm revenues in this country, they have increased in number by nearly 80 percent in the past ten years, with California's more than three hundred markets leading all the states (New York is a close second). One writer described the gathering of greengrocers in a square at the corner of Santa Barbara and Cota Streets as "a garden party on a grand scale—with an astonishing array of fresh produce, flowers, and plants from a hundred forty growers."

One of those growers is Tom Shepherd, a farmer from nearby Carpinteria who caters to professional and amateur chefs with his fresh herbs, mixed lettuces, and other gourmet items. A trend-spotter who studies food magazines and other resources to figure out what he should be planting in his fields, Shepherd invented his own solar drier when he saw that sun-dried tomatoes were becoming the rage a few years ago, and he introduced his own dried Herbes de Provence mix (thyme, rosemary, savory, sage, marjoram, and bay) when French cooking was hot. Long before the supermarket chains caught on to the appeal of mesclun salad, he was one of the first growers to offer it to the American market, and this Saturday morning at his booth he was still selling five-dollar plastic bags of the mix at a good clip.

Another successful niche farmer in Carpinteria is Jim Hipple, who came to California

below: A good example of successful niche farming is Jim Hipple's range of greenhouses in the Carpinteria hills, near Santa Barbara, devoted entirely to the cultivation of *Hydrangea macrophylla.* Grown in several varieties, the long-lasting white, pink, and blue blooms of hydrangea are much in demand by florists and designers.

opposite, clockwise from top left: Scenes from the Saturday-morning market in Santa Barbara: native blueberries and blackberries set out in eyecatching checkerboard pattern; flowers galore, including lavender in bloom, daisies, dahlias forced in pots, and towering delphiniums; new red and white potatoes the size of golf balls; and zucchini with blossoms still attached.

from the Midwest when his father bought a boatyard in Ventura. He grows several varieties of hydrangea (all in the genus *Hydrangea macrophylla*) in a range of greenhouses within view of his home. His market is primarily the florists and designers in presentation-conscious Southern California who value the long-lasting white, pink, and blue blooms of hydrangea for use in large bouquets and other decorations. Hipple grows his plants in large individual containers to better manage the feeding and watering tasks.

"The color of hydrangea can be altered between pink and blue by manipulating the amount of the element aluminum that the plant absorbs," he says, drawing on the formal training in ornamental horticulture he received at San Luis Obispo agricultural school, part of California Polytech. "Blue flowers are produced when you increase the plant's ability to absorb aluminum sulfate; pink flowers result from low availability of the same element."

California gardeners like Julia Rappaport of North Tustin, in Orange County, have long been concerned about the increasing disconnect between today's young citizens and the nation's rural traditions. Not only has she strongly supported the state's "A Garden in Every School" project for more than a decade, she has donated a portion of her two-acre garden to the avocado breeding program at the University of California, Riverside.

"Gardening began for me when I was teaching a combined fifth- and sixth-grade science class," she recalls. "I had seventy students in a brand-new school and no books or

materials to get started with. So we planted seventy feet of radishes and seventy feet of carrots, and the kids loved it."

Rappaport's own garden begins at her front walk with a collection of Monterey and Aleppo pines, underplanted with azaleas, rhododendrons, hellebores, and bulbs. "My garden is a gardener's garden," she says. "I grow plants that only other gardeners like to see," including bromeliads, clivia, Barbra Streisand and Iceberg roses, one hundred assorted fruit trees, and forty tomato plants. Not to mention a variety of avocado she herself developed, named Regal R in her honor.

Educating both children and adults about agriculture and California's farming heritage is the mission of Bell Gardens Farm in the Valley Center area of north San Diego County. Glen Bell Jr., the founder of the seven-thousand—strong Taco Bell chain of Mexican fast-food restaurants, established Bell Gardens in the fall of 1993 "to teach visitors about the art and science of growing fruits and vegetables, while encouraging the guardianship of our natural resources."

A working farm with more than 50 different crops on 115 acres, Bell Gardens is an open-air classroom, alive with lessons in adobe brick-making, the planting process, soils, irrigation, and the environment. Making school trips here such a delight for kids are child-friendly attractions like Ghost Canyon, a walking trail amid gnarled oaks; Corn Maize, a maze within a 1,000-square-foot cornfield; and an eighty-passenger quarter-scale train that meanders through the property.

Bell grew up on a ten-acre farm in the

below left and center: Bell Gardens Farm in San Diego County, a working farm with more than 50 crops on 115 acres, created and funded by the founder of Taco Bell, is designed as an open-air classroom, primarily for children, "to teach visitors about the art and science of growing fruits and vegetables, while encouraging the guardianship of our natural resources." Attractions include a 1,000-square-foot field of corn planted as a labyrinth, a miniature train, and a walking trail through gnarled oaks and other vegetation, called "Ghost Canyon." *opposite*: David Karle, manager of Bell Gardens Farm.

opposite, above left and right: Bougainvillea and other vines thrive on the walls, pillars, and portals of Mission San Juan Capistrano, while salvias, hollyhocks, and other blooms carpet the gardens. *opposite, below:* The courtyard of the 10-acre site is a popular gathering place, in this case the occasion being a fund-raiser by the Friends of the Mission. *below:* A view toward the ruins of the Great Stone Church.

San Bernardino Mountains during the Great Depression and knew both the challenge and value of being able to bring one's own crops to table. As a youngster, he and his siblings sold cut flowers door to door for extra money, and, in a preview of the entrepreneurial genius that would mark his business career, he teamed up with his great-aunt, Mary Dye, during berry season to bake twenty to thirty miniature fruit pies at a time. They sold them for ten cents apiece and split three thousand dollars in profit at summer's end.

The children's garden at Mission San Juan Capistrano is a relatively new addition to this historic church, the seventh in the California mission chain, known as the jewel in the chain. The church occupies a ten-acre site in the town of the same name, famous for the swallows that traditionally return to the area every spring. Towering hollyhocks and cascading bougainvillea stand out sharply against the earth tones of the arched walls in the central courtyard. A variety of water plants float on the waters of the fountain in the middle of the space. An herb garden planted in a cruciform shape adds a quiet spiritual note to the section reserved for kids.

Founded by Franciscan missionaries in 1776, the mission is a useful reminder that all California gardening began here and then. "They founded missions along, and within the protection of, mission walls, and created gardens with seeds brought from Mexico," writes Karen Dardick in *Estate Gardens of California*. "Important plants included olive trees for oil, grape vines for sacramental wine, cit-

rus, figs, dates, pomegranates, strawberries, raspberries, and other fruit for their refectory tables. There were also herbs, such as lavender for medicinal use, and flowers to decorate the altars."

The missions and their gardens have enjoyed and sometimes endured a checkered history over the years. But one city newly mindful of its past and one group of citizen volunteers with a passionate interest in restoring the city's most venerable spaces foretells a bright future for San Juan Capistrano. And a garden is in the middle of it.

2

PASSIONATE COLLECTORS

The most important object of a collection is the next one.

—PHILIPP BLOM, *To Have and to Hold: An Intimate History of Collectors and Collecting* (2003)

Like all enthusiasts, obsessive horticulturists must possess—not merely admire—the objects of their devotion. One of the great plant collectors of all time, John Tradescant the Elder lived in England in the late 16th and early 17th centuries. In his capacity as gardener to the Duke of Buckingham and, later, keeper of His Majesty's Gardens, Vines and Silkworms at Oatlands in Surrey, Tradescant made numerous foreign expeditions in search of novel specimens for the estates of his employers. (The North American native *Tradescantia,* among other plants, takes its name from this botanical explorer.) Among the plants and shrubs he introduced into the English landscape were the horse chestnut, lilac, plane tree, larch, acacia, tulip tree, and Virginia creeper.

Tradescant collected things as well as plants, in the fashion of his time, displaying them in "cabinets of curiosities." Three hundred years later, the financier J. P. Morgan, typifying a new breed of fabulously wealthy American collectors, "buying as if there were no tomorrow," notes Philipp Blom—in *To Have and to Hold,* a fascinating look at the many faces of collecting over the centuries—simply increased the scale of the cabinet to what is today the Pierpont Morgan Library, one of the world's greatest collections of works on paper. No wonder he felt free to decorate the East Room in his mansion with a Brussels tapestry, *The Triumph of Avarice.*

With mass production, collecting became accessible to people of less extravagant means than Morgan and his ilk. If the folks shambling onto the set of *Antiques Roadshow* with their musty treasures are any guide, the world of collecting has become democratized to a fault. "A man collects milk bottles 'because I saw that people were throwing them away,'" reports Blom. "Now he has thousands of them, classified according to origin and age, a British geography in milk bottles and a garden shed transformed."

Gardeners who collect plants tend to specialize in the exotic or the rare, whether they be hothouse orchids or winter-flowering irises, or carnivorous plants like the Venus flytrap or the pitcher plant, or the lost and forgotten cultivars that the "rose rustlers" of Texas seek out in old cemeteries or the overgrown yards of abandoned homes. (Plant collectors are zealots; the photographer Edward Steichen had such a passion for delphiniums, especially blue delphiniums, that he bred and collected them in his Connecticut garden into his nineties.)

top: Country folk art feels at home in the house of a gardener.
above: Ephemera on the arcane subject of reel-mower technology.
opposite: A bedroom is infused with the owner's love of gardening—and her terrier, Hildegarde.

Collectors of gardening things seem to be open to both the kitsch and the high culture of their objects of desire: the colorful seed packet in a twig frame, the original Redouté print in gilt. But they range as far afield as the plant collectors, if necessary, in search of that Haws watering can in mint condition, a bird feeder of distinction, an elegant cloche, a basket or vase worthy of the beautiful flowers in the cutting garden, plant labels as decorative as they are useful. Or it could be something they never dreamed of acquiring until they stumbled on it in a country flea market or a city antiques mall or a garage sale in the suburbs. If it speaks to their love of gardening, they will make a place for it, in the garden itself, or somewhere in the home as a reminder of the garden.

Romancing the Stones

"Urns" is one of those words which, if repeated over and over again, ceases to exist. It becomes a sort of mad braying in space. Urns. Urns. Urns. Urns. Urns.

—BEVERLEY NICHOLS, *Merry Hall* (1951)

The earliest rooms in Anne and Garrett Rowe's New Hampshire farmhouse date from 1800 and are suitably filled with a timeworn assortment of New England furnishings, but step through their back door, and you stumble into a field of antiquities that seem to place you in the Age of Pericles in Greece, or down the road from Vespasian's Colosseum in ancient Rome. For this is the holding area for the classically themed urns, vases, obelisks, fountains, arbors, benches, gates, sundials, armillary spheres, troughs, wall sinks, staddle stones, wheelbarrows, and sundry other, smaller garden furnishings, ornaments, implements, and tools that Anne brings back three or four times a year from buying trips in England.

Anne has been dealing in garden antiques, both old and not-so-old, and in such garden-oriented paraphernalia as folky gnomes, weathervanes, and edging tiles, for more than twenty-five years, but she is as much a collector of garden things as she is a dealer. Some of this material has never reached any of her many loyal clients up and down the eastern seaboard, for she has held back favorite pieces to lend structure and style to her own gardens, which surround the house in New Hampshire.

opposite: The Three Graces, a classically themed trio Anne Rowe found in England, is surrounded by turtlehead in Anne and Garrett Rowe's New Hampshire garden.

pair of guard-"dog" geese—aggressive birds that keep the yard free of interlopers from the surrounding woodlands—summer is a wonderful time to see their place in its natural splendor, and to observe how Anne has incorporated artifacts from her travels into her garden design: a small obelisk in a stand of lacy meadow rue; a stone carving of the Three Graces in the embrace of flowering turtlehead; a glowering warlock, fashioned from concrete, atop a stone wall; a sign she found at the New England Flower Show one year hanging from one of the garden sheds that her husband, a building contractor by trade, made for her. Embellished with a quote from Emerson, it reads "THE EARTH LAUGHS IN FLOWERS," and Anne's gardens, as well as her personality and spirit, corroborate the sentiment.

above: The oldest parts of the Rowe house date from around 1800. *right:* Anne Rowe's pet geese are "wonderful watch dogs," she says. "Nothing gets past them at night."

Her office in the barn next to the house shows off collections of plant pots, including "thumb pots" for starting seed, wire flower frogs in all sizes, and old salesman's samples of garden tools—miniature versions of spade forks, rakes, and hoes. On the sideboard in her dining room is a stack of first editions of the work of Gertrude Jekyll, the revered early-20th-century English garden writer, "whose wonderful information," says Anne, "is timeless."

Outside, if one can get by the Rowes'

It all began, Anne recalls, with a desire to contribute financially to the household and still be a stay-at-home mother. She was sitting in her kitchen, gazing at the youngest of her four children, Sarah, who was in a high chair at the time, and thinking there must be some kind of business she could operate from home. And dealing in antiques, a field she was always interested in, immediately sprang to mind.

"I made my first buying trip to England during the Queen's silver jubilee, almost thirty years ago now," she recalls. "I got off the plane and just fell in love with the place."

She met a friend in the cathedral city of Peterborough, north of London, and the two of them motored through the countryside, looking for shops, propelled by word of mouth from one town to the next. At first Anne collected small painted country furnishings and other items that would fit in suitcases. But her lifelong interest in gardening, as well as America's growing passion for the gardening life, caused her to shift gears, and soon she included architectural salvage yards on her English itinerary. "I still buy and sell country things," she says, "but the bulk of my business is in things for and about the garden."

Although today she buys in quantities and sizes that require 40-foot-long shipping containers, rather than suitcases, to get her acquisitions home, she professes to keep her buying and selling philosophy realistic.

top left: In the dining room, Anne Rowe displays her first editions by the eminent garden writer Gertrude Jekyll, collected on buying trips to England. The old watering can was given to her by a friend. *above and at left:* Anne's office in the barn is filled with gardening collectibles, including thumb pots for starting plants from seed, salesman's samples of garden tools, and a pair of utensils made of ivory and silver. *overleaf:* The perennial garden features a birdhouse and fences made by builder Garrett Rowe and a pathway by landscape designer Dan Wheeler.

"I don't deal in huge, expensive statuary," she declares. "I love what is accessible to people. I love simple, utilitarian objects like an old watering can or trug (a flat basket for transporting cut flowers), a quaint birdbath, or an unusual garden tool. Things that are practical yet have been made with a note of grace and beauty. That's what my customers and I respond to."

Although the origin of garden accoutrements can be traced to many cultures and ages, it is generally agreed that, in the West at least, Renaissance Italy surpassed all others in fully integrating architectural elements and furnishings into the landscape of the garden. As Nellie Doubleday, an early-20th-century American garden writer put it in a 1908 issue of the magazine *Country Life in America,* Lorenzo de Medici's Florentine garden, with its broad paths, pergolas and pools, garden seats, urns and balustrades, represented "garden craft carried to its highest degree."

Inspired by the Italians, the garden designers of France, Spain, and Holland, among others, took up the cause, adding their own native wrinkles. The prosperity and creativity of Elizabethan and Victorian England fostered even richer variations on the theme. Country life remains the soul of Britain even to this day, and country gar-

right: On buying trips abroad, dealer Anne Rowe keeps her eye out for "what any gardener would want to use and have." *far right:* The sign in the entry came from Maine by way of a friend in the antiques business; wooden barrels store pet food, bird seed, and root vegetables.

dens have always stood as the external manifestation of the British dream of an orderly and sociable Eden. Blessed with a climate to make all things verdant, the English country garden (attached to an English country home) truly came into its own in the 19th century. A wealthy middle class had time on its hands. The newly invented lawn mower was a vast improvement over the scythe for converting idle acreage into close-cropped sporting venues. Indeed the domestic lawnmower put the "lawn" into lawn tennis. Badminton, quoits, and above all croquet were other uniquely English games that competed for space with gardens.

According to *Cassell's Book of Sports and Pastimes,* published circa 1900, croquet "was productive of what may be almost called a revolution in the social life of the country; for from the time of its recognition as a national game, garden parties, which had hitherto been very dull and monotonous affairs, became the most common and popular of all entertainments in country places."

While croquet faded, gardening endured in the world of English country. And even while that world represents influences both home-grown and imported, from China and Japan as well as from Europe, the English garden has been the prototype for most American gardeners, ever since Colonial times; English experts on gardening, such as Gerturde Jekyll, have been our preachers. That mystique is what makes the materials that pile up in Anne Rowe's holding area in New Hampshire, no matter where they came from originally, such objects of desire.

above: The early American painted pine table was one of the first things Anne and Garrett acquired after marrying. The onion-pattern Meissen china in the corner cupboard belonged to Garrett's grandparents. English and French watering cans occupy the window seat.

A Classic Garden Library

Dirty fingernails are not the only requirement for growing plants. One must be as willing to study as to dig, for a knowledge of plants is acquired as much from books as from experience.

—ELIZABETH LAWRENCE, *A Southern Garden* (1942)

Books have been an inspiration to gardeners for almost as long as the printed word itself. Few collections of such titles can match the depth and breadth of the library of the Massachusetts Horticultural Society, but fascination with garden volumes dates from Colonial times. Among our founding fathers, Thomas Jefferson relied on garden books, when he wasn't writing them himself, as well as extensive travel, to design and plant the landscapes at Monticello and, later, at the University of Virginia. Much more of a homebody, George Washington leaned heavily on his collection of imported books on agronomy, animal husbandry, and horticulture to develop his comprehensive vision for agriculture in the New World at Mount Vernon.

"He read widely in his garden books, mastered the subject as laid out in them for English and French landholders of means and resources, and proceeded to lay out his own garden of exactly the appropriate size and style for his manor house," observes Diane Kostial McGuire in *Keeping Eden: A History of Gardening in America.* "Nowhere did he overstep, overdo, overdesign, or overbuild."

opposite: Before moving to its new headquarters, the library of the Massachusetts Horticultural Society housed more than 85,000 garden books in the august, neoclassical Horticultural Hall in the heart of Boston.

above: **Before the advent of photography, garden books relied on superior design, inside and out, to captivate the eye of the reader. MassHort's collection contains thousands of exquisite examples.**

How-not-to-garden books and, increasingly, magazines, which also became a staple of personal garden libraries, flourished in the United States in the late 19th and early 20th centuries. With *The Horticulturist,* founded in 1846, Andrew Jackson Downing, the editor and proselytizer of a newly minted country life style, raised writing about gardening to a new level. Following in his footsteps, such magazines as *Better Homes and Gardens, Woman's Home Companion, Country Life in America, The Garden Magazine,* and *The House Beautiful* supplied a burgeoning middle class with information on how to make both more beautiful and more practical garden spaces for their country and suburban dwellings.

Describing the pre–World War II era as "the golden age of garden writing" in America, Virginia Tuttle Clayton observed in her book *The Once & Future Garden* (2000), that the contributors to these magazines were a varied lot: academics, architects, clergymen, sociologists, artists, photographers, writers, editors, dietitians, and librarians, as well as landscape architects and designers. "Prompted by the moralistic, reforming spirit of . . . current movements," Clayton noted, "they felt an obligation to educate and uplift those as yet unacquainted with these refining influences; with magazines as a powerful pulpit, their ideas subsequently infiltrated the rest of American society."

For a century and a half the "MassHort" garden library was housed in Horticultural Hall, one of the country's most imposing neoclassical buildings, directly across the street from Symphony Hall in Boston. Recently moved to modern quarters in Wellesley, the library, established in 1829, holds more than 85,000 garden books, magazines, and catalogs, and serves the research needs and interests not only of its 10,000 members but scholars, historians, and the general gardening public.

Portraits of the patrician males hanging throughout Horticultural Hall are pertinent reminders of the wealthy and socially prominent merchants, manufacturers, financiers, and professionals who dominated not just MassHort but all the horticultural societies that formed in the United States in the 19th century. While nurserymen, seedsmen, and practical gardeners had a hand in supervising the exhibitions that these societies sponsored to promote healthy competition among gardeners, the dead-white-male factor controlled all the important offices and set the tone. Women gardeners did not gain significant influence in such groups until after the Civil War.

These early horticultural bluebloods had more than a superficial interest in gardening, however. In fact, according to social historian Tamara Plakins Thornton, in the essay "Horticulture and the Ameri-

can Character," appearing in *Keeping Eden*, they gardened with a vengeance.

"The new taste for gardening was touted as proof that America's millionaires had in fact risen above the drive for riches," Thornton writes. "Horticultural gatherings thus became orgies of self-congratulation, at which participants toasted each other on their mutual achievement of moral purity and cultural refinement."

For all their pretensions, the movers and shakers behind the country's early horticultural societies created programs that have done an infinite amount of good in the world of gardening. The library of the Massachusetts Horticultural Society alone represents a database that gardeners of every variety can access and enjoy.

above: In addition to garden books, the library at MassHort, founded in 1829, has numerous examples of early seed catalogs and garden-related publications and reference works.

Floral Folk

*The pedigree of honey does not concern the bee—
a clover, any time, to him, is aristocracy.*

—EMILY DICKINSON, "THE PEDIGREE OF HONEY" (C. 1884)

Texas pedigree imbues the collections of former English teacher and Emily Dickinson fan Harold Hollis, a fact that is captured most emphatically by the numerous bluebonnet paintings that grace the walls of the home he has fashioned out of a 1960-built bunkhouse barn. Sunday bluebonnet painters are a dime a dozen in Texas, especially in early spring when this wildflower of the lupine family turns a north-south corridor of central Texas, with the city of Austin more or less at the center, into oceans of blue and draws thousands of gawkers onto country roads. The most esteemed among contemporary painters of bluebonnet scenes, however, fetch for a single canvas prices upward of five thousand dollars.

"No one mistakes bluebonnet paintings for high art," says Hollis, "but there is an inherent charm in the work that native Texans respond to." The often formulaic treatment in such a painting, with the obligatory wandering path, the stout live oak tree, a patch of cactus in bloom, perhaps a stretch of barbed-wire fence, and, always, hazy hills in the background, is as satisfying as comfort food. The various shades of blue among the six recognized species of the flower are often depicted in combination with other native wildflowers—the creamy orange and red of Indian paint-

opposite: Colorful pottery made for the tourist trade in Tlaquepaque, Mexico, includes nested chickens and turtles. The concrete birdbath, with a base made to resemble a tree trunk, comes from East Texas. A tiny bluebonnet landscape, painted on plywood cut in the shape of the Lone Star State, hangs on the wall.

below: Harold Hollis is an ardent gardener, nurturing native plant varieties through a nine-month-long growing season. *bottom left:* Harold's welcoming front porch, with flower pots and strawberry pots from the Byrd Pottery in East Texas. *bottom right:* The bottlebrush, a shrub of the genus *Callistemon.*

brush; the lavender, pink, white, and red blooms of Drummond's phlox; the pink of buttercups; the fiery purple of winecups; and the rusty red-and-yellow pinwheels of summer-flowering Indian blanket.

"Our wildflower meadows are really pretty in the spring, especially when we have had adequate rainfall the previous fall," Harold observes. "People pull their cars off the road and walk out into the fields for their photo ops. Part of the appeal is the joy of spring itself and the realization that new life is coming to the land. And part is our pride in our native flowers."

Official interest in bluebonnets dates back to 1901, when *Lupinus subcarnosus* was voted in as the state flower by the Texas legislature, narrowly beating out the cotton boll and the cactus flower. "The person most responsible for Texans' obsession with bluebonnet paintings," writes Skip Hollandsworth in the March 1997 issue of *Texas Monthly,* "was an artist named Julian Onderdonk, whose father, San Antonio painter Robert Onderdonk, had made a name for himself with such epic works as *The Fall of the Alamo.* . . . Like his father, Julian got his training at art schools in New York. When the young man returned to Texas in 1909, he decided to apply the newly popular French Impressionistic style of painting to Texas landscapes, using a fusion of dreamy color, putting a haze over the hills, adding streaks of pink and gray to the sky, and blending in a glorious field of bluebonnets across a

valley." Memorializing the bluebonnet in pictorial form became even more fashionable after the occasion of the state's centennial year of 1936 placed the colorful traditions and customs of Texas and Texans in the spotlight as never before.

It is not surprising that Harold would have an abiding interest in Texas history. The Hollis side of his family emigrated from Alabama to East Texas just before 1900. The maternal side, name of Benfer, settled in Harris County, where Houston is located, in 1866. His mother's family name is one of only five listed on the historical marker for the town of Klein, which at one time was separate from Houston but has since been annexed. Harold is currently researching the life and career of one Caleb Ives, an Episcopal clergyman and educator reared in Vermont who established the first academy in what was then the Republic of Texas in the 1840s. He had previously spent five years as a priest in Alabama, in an

area known as the Canebrake, near Birmingham, Tuscaloosa, and Mobile. "His diary, which I hope to see published one day," says Hollis, "is a fascinating glimpse into life on the Texas frontier."

Ironically, when Harold began collecting seriously three decades ago, he was attracted to traditional New England antiques such as baskets, painted furniture, and hooked rugs. "Sometimes you grow up loving things, as I did our wildflowers," admits Hollis, "but taking them for granted, and the same was true for other aspects of Texas culture that were so familiar to me, such as the rich ranching traditions in my own family."

above left: Vases painted with bluebonnet scenes were popular souvenirs from the 1920s to the '40s. *above:* The bluebonnet painting above the cupboard is signed by Lucy R. Hall. Next to it, a painting with a road and a church dates from the 1940s. The oil-on-canvas watermelon was painted in the 1920s. Below is an unsigned oil-on-board rendering of sharecroppers, originally from Alabama. The watermelon on the Texas German Biedermeier table is Mexican pottery.

Meanwhile, he became intrigued with the severe New England sensibility of Emily Dickinson, whose work he studied in graduate school at Southern Methodist University, and the more accessible por-

tions of which he later used as a classroom teacher. It was not until the mid-1980s, long after he had left teaching to enter the business world, that he had the chance to visit her Amherst, Massachusetts, home. Although he says he is still "often puzzled by her secrets, her complex allusions," he believes she was much less of a recluse than people think, and, indeed, her letters bear out her engagement in the world and particularly her profound awareness of the life in the natural world. She had her own herbarium at one point—"'most all the girls are making one," she wrote a friend. In August 1861 she wrote to Mrs. Samuel Bowles (wife of the editor of the Springfield *Republican*), "How is your garden, Mary? Are all the pinks true, and the sweet williams faithful? I've got a geranium like a sultana, and when the humming-birds come down, geranium and I shut our eyes, and go far away."

Although Harold remains an admirer of Dickinson, "around 1984 it dawned on me that New England was not my heritage and that what I really wanted to collect was Texana, and since then I have largely replaced all my New England finds with things, mostly from the 19th and early 20th century, that reflect the Anglo, Czech, Polish, Hispanic, and black cultures, all of which have long and rich traditions in the state."

Located on his family's two-hundred-acre property in the post oak savannah lands of east central Texas, Harold's house has been furnished and decorated with the deliberate aim of reflecting the diverse ethnic strains found within the Lone Star State: a Biedermeier table with its original finish, from a German dogtrot farmhouse in Cat Spring; a stretcher-base table with lift-off top from a Polish family who farmed near Schulenburg in the 1870s; and a late-19th-century Czech cupboard with floral cutouts from Moulton coexist happily in his eclectic mix. For western trappings, he has included a spool bed made of mesquite, a dozen cowhide-seated chairs made in Crockett, and a few "duded-up" 10-gallon hats. A primitive oil-on-board painting, depicting two black sharecroppers picking cotton, with their one-room house in the background, graces one wall,

below: A 19th-century mesquite bed found at a garage sale in LaGrange, Texas, is clad in a quilt given to Harold Hollis by his aunt Edna Fuchs and made by her mother, Emily Rustenbach. The hooked rug with a rooster dates from the late 19th century. The rug with an abstract floral design came from Vermont, while the rug on the floor, with a basket of tulips, was found in South Hadley, Massachusetts. On the table, a tin bowl of beaded fruit, made as a cottage craft from the 1930s to '50s, is companionably joined by a terra-cotta pineapple from Mexico. The horn bench was a popular item in western states in the late 19th century.

top and above: Painted trays and lacquered boxes with landscapes and flowers were made in Michoacan, Mexico, in the 1920s. A compote made from Popsicle sticks holds gourds that have been painted to look like fruit. The primitive oil-on-board still-life dates from the early 20th century.

and floral-painted vases from various potteries, especially the famous Meyer Pottery, which flourished in the San Antonio area from the 1920s to the 1940s, as well as colorful souvenir turtles and nested chickens made for the tourist trade in Tlaquepaque, Mexico, are among the accessories.

The gardens Hollis has built around his house feature plants native or naturalized to the Texas ecosystem and include sages, salvias, cactus, desert willow, artemesia, ornamental grasses, and many other varieties. "My garden, like my collection, is a work in progress," he says, "but I definitely like stuff that gives me payback over our nine-month growing season. I like repeat bloomers," like his bottlebrush plants, which flower from spring to late fall, and his old garden roses, which bloom continuously from early spring to December.

Harold has collected bluebonnet paintings on canvases and boards cut in the distinctive shape of the state of Texas, and they are among his favorite folk art. But bluebonnets do not grow universally well in the state, which after all spans four hardiness zones and receives annual rainfall in amounts as little as 8 inches in El Paso and as much as 56 inches along the Louisiana border. Texas gardeners often choose coneflowers, coreopsis, and black-eyed Susans to substitute for bluebonnets in regions with growing conditions that differ dramatically from the Hill Country, and thus the heavenly blues of the flower do not spread uniformly across the land. Compromise is inevitable in gardening, but as Harold Hollis can attest, painted images of flowers and landscapes, especially those with Texas pedigree, will dull the pain.

Paradise Contained

The love of flowers is a sentiment common alike to the great and to the little; to the old and to the young; to the learned and the ignorant; the illustrious and the obscure. While the simplest child may take delight in them, they may also prove a recreation to the most profound philosophers.

—ELIZABETH KENT, *Flora Domestica* (1823)

opposite: A cloche for tender plants is used to create a moist terrarium atmosphere for an African violet growing in an antique English hand-thrown pot. The water-color of a rose in the background was painted by an unknown 19th-century artist.

One of the books in coauthor Kathryn Precourt's garden library is a reproduction of the famous *Besler Florilegium,* published in two volumes in 1613. A spectacular documentation of the Nuremberg, Germany, apothecary of Basil Besler, it contains hand-colored engraved plates and etchings of some 1,000 flowers and 667 species, organized by season.

"The book describes a collection of flowers all cultivated in a single garden, that of a German nobleman," says Precourt, "but to me it's a reminder of the richness and variety underfoot in just about anyone's garden."

That goes for the set of gardens Kathryn has been developing over the past decade on the gently sloping terrain behind the house she and her husband, Geoffrey, occupy in the foothills of the Berkshires in western Massachusetts. Remnants of the apple orchard original to the site are still in place, with young fruit trees added to perpetuate

spring to fall, seems to create a new garden each and every growing season) are dedicated to individual species such as hosta, daylilies, peonies, and in a single circular bed, poppies and lupines of many hues.

A lifelong collector, as is her husband (whose manias include first editions of American novelists, vintage cocktail shakers, and Boston Red Sox memorabilia), Kathryn draws on her antique glass and ceramic vessels, including 19th-century English lusterware and relief-molded pitchers, to create her own ever-changing florilegium of bouquets from the garden for her house. From forcing forsythia, quince, dogwood, spirea, pussy willow, and fruit branches in the spring, to harvesting from the wild landscape in her rural area in the late summer and fall, filling vases with Queen Anne's lace, milkweed, meadowsweet, wild mint, cattails, goldenrod, and other bounty from roadside and pasture, Precourt practices the

the tradition, in spite of incursions by whitetail deer and one mournful-looking moose who seems to have wandered down from Maine by mistake.

Raised beds built into the slope hold the homeowner's sundry vegetable crops, while a stone terrace directly under her kitchen window, enclosed with a white picket fence, hosts culinary herbs and choice perennial flowers and shrubs. For an annual spring treat, a nearby wooded hillside has been planted with five thousand narcissus bulbs. Other garden areas (and Precourt, a tireless hands-on gardener from

art of paradise collected and contained.

"Almost anything can be used as a container for flowers," she observes, and a storage room in her basement overflows with goblets, bowls, carafes, fine hand-blown crystal, old perfume bottles, dozens of bud vases, and boxes and trugs for forcing crocus, narcissus, hyacinths, and tulips in the last months of the long New England winter when such blooms warm and animate any room with their smiling grace. She finds containers at tag sales, flea markets, antiques fairs, and antiques shops, seldom paying more than a song for them.

She also has a special talent for locating stylish picture frames in the piles of junk often passing for bargains at flea markets, and these come in handy for showing off the botanical art that Kathryn and Geoffrey also collect. Not to be confused with painted flowers, but equally graphic, dried and pressed botanical specimens from the late 19th century adorn one wall of their master bedroom, while Victorian tinsel paintings of flowers hang above the bed in the guest room. Still more floral patterns are found in Precourt's collections of blue-and-white china, arranged above a dry sink in the dining room, and in her vintage fabrics, including colorful chintzes and toiles depicting rural scenes. Even a collection of buttons,

mounted on boards, has a floral motif.

The tradition of botanical illustration started long before Basil Besler, with evidence of such artwork, usually in connection with medical treatises or treatments, found in ancient China, Egypt, and Greece. For fifteen centuries, the definitive reference work on botany was *De materia medica* by the first-century A.D. Greek physician Dioscorides. A beautifully illustrated copy of this work, dating from A.D. 512 and containing closely observed watercolor drawings of medicinal plants, still exists in the National Library of Austria in Vienna. During the Middle Ages, the *Books of Hours* used for prayer and meditation were illuminated with renderings of plant and animal life. Books called herbals were another product of monastic life and also depicted the common healing plants.

Adventurous naturalists of the 18th century were the first to record in detail the exotic flora and fauna of the New World. Englishman Mark Catesby compiled his *The Natural History of Carolina, Florida,*

opposite, top: After a long New England winter, blossoms are a welcome sign of spring. *opposite, below:* Beaded, wax, and marble fruit are arrayed in front of a Chinese botanical. *above left:* An 18th-century Wedgwood gelatin mold rests on a 19th-century Leedsware platter. *above:* A spring bouquet of lilacs with tulips. *overleaf:* The botanicals in the Precourts' city apartment were found in flea markets. On the mantel, dried coxcomb has been arranged in antique cast-iron urns, often used at gravesites.

right: Three varieties of tulips interspersed with variegated hosta leaves are gathered in a late-19th-century English mug with an agricultural theme.

above: A collection of antique English luster-ware, many floral in pattern. *right:* The blue dry sink and shelf shows off a collection of antique delft, English transferware, and flow blue china. A 19th-century English Peking pitcher holds hydrangea, coneflowers, dahlias, and roses.

and the Bahama Islands (1731) in two heavily illustrated volumes, and Frenchman Andre Michaux produced *Flora Boreali—Americana* (1803), with many illustrations by the Belgian-born Pierre-Joseph Redouté, perhaps the most celebrated botanical artist of all. Redouté is best known for his portfolios of lilies and irises, as well as his renderings of roses from the garden of Josephine Bonaparte.

Although known primarily for his naturalistic paintings of birds, the American artist John James Audubon set his avian portraits among accurate depictions of many native American trees, shrubs, vines, and flowers in his monumental work, *The Birds of America,* among them mountain laurel and live oak.

Although commercial botanical illustration largely gave way to artful color photography in the 20th century, the tradition of drawing from nature is far from moribund. Beverly Duncan, who lives in the same town as the Precourts, is a self-taught botanical artist whose work has been widely published and exhibited in galleries; the famed Hunt Institute for Botanical Documentation in Pittsburgh has acquired several of her drawings. "She brings such acute observation to every rip and mottling that her fragile subjects have an intense individuality," wrote Kim Waller in *Victoria Magazine* (November 2002). Starting with pencil sketches from nature, Duncan paints her finished botanicals, warts and all. Those accurately rendered imperfections are what appeals to Precourt about Duncan's work.

"I've enjoyed trying to match up my own arrangements with the flowers that appear in Beverly's work," says Kathryn. "When the combination clicks, there's a wonderful feeling of life imitating art, or the other way around."

top: In the guest bedroom are examples of Victorian tinsel pictures and a shadow box containing a bouquet fashioned from wool. Even the framed buttons have a floral motif. *above:* The flowering bulb *Galanthus,* or snowdrop, as rendered by the 19th-century *Cyclopedia of American Horticulture* and by contemporary artist Beverly Duncan.

Their Plates Runneth Over

When he wasn't with women he was collecting china.
Paying any price for both I understand.

—EDITH WHARTON, *The Age of Innocence* (1920)

The word *Staffordshire* is bandied about at flea markets as a generic term for any china made in England. In fact, it describes the artistic output of a specific English county, centered around Stoke-on-Trent in the Midlands. Rich in clay beds and deposits of the coal needed to fire its kilns, and easily reached by rail, the area first came to prominence in the 18th century as the center of English ceramic production, turning out massive amounts of both earthenware and, later, porcelain, primarily for domestic consumption, but also for export to the colonies.

The invention of transfer printing in 1753 enabled Staffordshire potters to produce copiously decorated wares on a mass scale. By 1795 there were 150 separate factories in the county, including such now famous names as Minton, Spode, and Wedgwood, all turning out dishware of all shapes, sizes, and colors, and numerous other eminently beautiful and breakable objects, such as animal figures, vases, and candlesticks. By the 19th century, Staffordshire was pouring into the United States; one ship alone carried 262,000 pieces to a china broker in Philadelphia.

While floral and botanical patterns are not unique to Staffordshire china, they present a recurring theme in its history, and they are found throughout the vast selection of antique wares on exhibit in the barn next to the 1776 Colonial house of deal-

opposite: The use of flowers and foliage for china patterns, both in naturalistic and fanciful renderings, is almost as old as pottery itself.

above: **The soup tureen and platter from Wedgwood features an elegant water lily pattern and luminescent tones of blue. This particular pattern was manufactured in 1811.**

ers Ann and Dennis Berard in Fitzwilliam, New Hampshire. "The intrinsic beauty of flowers made it a natural motif for Staffordshire, which was the CorningWare of its day," notes Dennis, who with his wife has specialized in Staffordshire china for more than fifteen years, both as a collector himself and as a dealer.

The chrysanthemum was probably the first flower to appear on a plate, because the Chinese, who were the first to make porcelain in the 7th and 8th centuries, held that blossom in especially high favor.

Although the Chinese have been exporting porcelain to the West since the 16th century, European craftsmen did not begin mimicking their techniques until the 18th century, first in Meissen, Germany, and Sevres, France, and finally in England. In all three countries the floral pattern of choice was the rose.

clockwise from left: A forget-me-not frog mug made by Gaudy Welch, circa 1840. A lavender rose pattern from around 1820. Sugar bowls made between 1820 and 1840. A black transferware pitcher and bowl in the Imperial fruit pattern, made by T. Mayer Stoke, circa 1830.

Pressed to Paper

As a means of enlarging and disciplining the mind, training it to habits of correct observation and profitable reflection, the Study of Plants is far superior to any of those fashionable and fugitive attainments which now so frequently engross the attention of the young.

—DR. WILLIAM DARLINGTON, *First Lessons in Botany* (1851)

Some gardening collections reflect the garden universe with a totality that is at once awesome and intimate. Such is the case with the botanical specimens and other images of plant life that David Winter has amassed. His carefully preserved and presented vestiges of the natural world grace the walls of his Brooklyn apartment and Manhattan gallery, "as art, if you will," in his own words, "created quite inadvertently by both scientists and enthusiasts of nature unadorned."

Winter's infatuation with this accidental art form itself came about as an accident. Trained as a sculptor, he had stopped in at a preview of a general book auction at Swann Gallery in New York City, in 1992, in hopes of finding prints by Piranesi or other artists whose work related to his interest in sculpture.

"By chance, I opened an oversized leather-bound volume and was shocked to be

opposite: David Winter's Manhattan gallery, Winter Works on Paper, features a wide range of dried, pressed, and mounted plant specimens, nature prints, and photograms, as well as vintage posters and photographs.

right: A page from an herbarium documenting the flora of the Holy Land, a popular locale for botanizers at the turn of the 20th century.

above: Cyanotype photograms by an anonymous 19th-century English collector relied on a technique that was a variant of the sun print; the dried and pressed plant specimen was placed on paper coated with chemicals, which burned the image of the plant onto the paper.

looking at a real blade of grass," he recalls. The volume was an herbarium, a collection of dried, pressed, and mounted plant specimens that in this instance had been bound in book form and published, complete with typeset captions.

"The illustrations were the plants themselves," he relates. "I found that a blade of grass, flattened and isolated on the page, had tremendous graphic power." *Hortus Gramineus Woburnensis* had been produced in 1816 by George Sinclair, gardener to the Duke of Bedford in England, as a horticul-

tural guide to grasses for farmers, "but it had all the power of a book of art."

Smitten, Winter won the Sinclair book at auction and then began his search for more specimens, which continues to this day. Along the way he discovered a variation on the herbarium, in the form of the 1855 botanical classic *Ferns of Great Britain and Ireland,* by Thomas Moore with illustrations by Henry Bradbury. Rather than actual plants, this book featured images made through a technique called electrotype nature printing, in which real ferns were pressed directly into a soft metal plate, from which, after the plate hardened, multiple images could be struck. This was an improvement upon an earlier copying method, in which an image is made by inking the plant itself and pressing it directly to paper.

"The technique produces an image that is a near-perfect replication of the plant—worm holes, broken bits, and all," he notes. "Unlike most botanical illustration, which tends to idealize the plant, nature printing shocks us with its veracity."

In time, after building a comprehensive collection of dried and mounted botanical specimens and nature prints, David expanded his search to include botanical photograms, or sun prints—images made by placing plants on photosensitive paper and exposing them to sunlight. Pioneering this technique was the brilliant scientist (and avid horticulturalist) William Henry Fox Talbot, Winter reports. "He made extraordinary sun pictures that were soft-edged, impressionistic, and sometimes delicately colored in shades of lavender, sepia, rose, and chartreuse." When Talbot published a collection of these images in his book *The Pencil of Nature,* which came out serially during 1844 and 1845, it became the first book ever to be illustrated with photographs and thus an instant milestone in the history of photography.

Having inadvertently discovered the romance of botanical collecting, Winter opened a gallery to serve that interest, as well as to carry the vintage photographs and posters he had also become interested in. But perhaps his greatest contribution to understanding the artistic merit of botanical specimens, nature prints, and photograms has been the publication, in 1999, of *The Pressed Plant,* a lavishly illustrated volume he produced with the writer Andrea DiNoto. The book celebrates the astonishing beauty of diverse yet related botanical images, all of which are, or have been made from, actual plants.

below: A plate from an 1874 book by the German printmaker Hieronymous Kniphof. *bottom left:* A plate from an album made in India in the 1870s; behind it, a plate from George Sinclair's *Gramineus Wobornensis,* 1816. *right:* A painting by David Winter hangs in his apartment.

The Pressed Plant also introduces readers to the passionate plant people behind the images. From as early as the 16th century, wealthy individuals, commercial growers, and botanical societies hired plant hunters from England and Western Europe to roam the world in search of new plant varieties. Careful documentation of each plant species was considered essential, so the hunters were required to dry and label every variety they discovered before shipping their findings home. To this day, according to Winter, there are three-hundred-year-old dried and mounted specimens in excellent condition in many institutional collections.

Bringing back live plants and seeds intact and viable was another matter, for untold hazards attended such commodities at sea. The invention of the terrarium (originally known as the Wardian case) in 1834 by Nathaniel B. Ward, an amateur naturalist in London, greatly improved the odds for survival, after which plant curiosities were successfully retrieved from the wild in quantities never before achieved.

The New World was ripe territory for botanizing adventurers. The first home-grown plant scholar in the colonies, according to Winter, was John Bartram, a Pennsylvania Quaker born in 1699, who supplied numerous English estate gardens, as well as the eminent Swedish naturalist Carolus Linnaeus (creator of the first universal system for naming plants) with new plants over more than four decades. In addition, Bartram and his sons indentified and introduced into cultivation more than two hundred native plants, including such familiar species as the magnolia, redbud, climbing honeysuckle, and Venus's flytrap. (Now named Bartram's Garden, the 18th-century site in Philadelphia is still intact and open to the public.)

By the early 19th century, the rapidly evolving field of natural history had attracted numerous amateur plant collectors into the fold. Collecting clubs were formed along with networks for exchange of specimens. Educated women of America's new and growing leisure class embraced the hobby with a passion. "Botanizers found innocent pleasure and glowing cheeks in going out into nature to discover, identify, and press plants," Winter observes, "and they filled the Sunday landscape." Indeed, some of the more zealous female botanizers of the day made significant contributions to the science. Kate Furbish of Brunswick, Maine, for example, gathered and catalogued the plants of her native state until she was ninety. Her collection of four thousand dried plants from all corners of Maine is now part of Harvard's Gray Herbarium.

The techniques of botanizing are well within the grasp of ordinary gardeners today, Winter says. "You may wish to create an ongoing herbarium record of your own garden," he suggests, "including examples of new plants added each year. Or you may want to create framed specimens for your home, or use pressed plants as elements in a travel diary." (Winter adds the caveat that the National Park Service

and many state and local parks forbid the collecting of specimens without permission; he recommends that collectors also obtain any one of several published guides to endangered plant species.)

At the heart of the impulse to botanize, and thereby to preserve, is a love affair with the plant itself. As Winter and DiNoto conclude in *The Pressed Plant*: "What we see . . . is that the plant itself remains the most provocative of symbols, a talisman of this earth's eternal truths, beauties, and mysteries."

above: The framed fern over the sofa is from the last and most lavish nature-printed book made by Henry Bradbury in 1855. The vintage scarecrow on the bookcase is from New Hampshire. *opposite, above:* Herbariums compiled by 19th-century botanizers in Switzerland and the United States. *opposite, below:* David Winter at work at home.

Lawn Mower Man

The flower garden on turf requires a neat and practiced mower to keep it short, by cutting it at least once a fortnight; for upon the shortness and closeness of the lawn the good effect of the flower garden largely depends.

—ANDREW JACKSON DOWNING, *Victorian Cottage Residences* (1842)

opposite: The typical reel mower has five blades that cut the grass like scissors when they come in contact with the stationary "bed knife." The average blade width is 16 inches, while the narrowest, used for trimming, is about 6 inches.

Jim Ricci's garage next to his home in western Massachusetts is filled with guy things, as might be expected of a place belonging to a skilled do-it-yourselfer with a background in remodeling houses and rebuilding engines in a machine shop. But if you step—carefully—inside the building, and pick your way among the clutter occupying both levels, you soon realize you are in the presence of a one-note collection of objects all devoted to a singularly male preoccupation: mowing the American lawn, of which, currently, there are 25 million acres.

Everywhere in piles on the floor or stacked loosely in overhead bins or arranged on broad benches, with their handles jutting out like cellos in an orchestra pit, are mechanical reel mowers, some dating back to the 1870s, with names like Peerless and Ideal and Excelsior and Easy. Ricci has collected more than five hundred of them, paying "more than I ever wanted to tell anyone" for some at tag sales, flea markets, and antiques shops, and receiving others gratis from friends and neighbors clearing out their own garages.

Inspired Plantsmen, Passionate Collectors, and Singular Visions in the World of Gardening

Philadelphia Lawn Mower Company, Inc.

Philadelphia
lawn mower
Style-A

SPECIFICATIONS

Height of Drive Wheels............................10 inches
Diameter of Revolving Cutter.............6½ inches
Number of Blades...........................5
Kind of Bearings...........................Adjustable Bushings
Bearing............................Single Train

LIST PRICES

15 inch....................$30.00
17 inch....................34.00
19 inch....................38.00
21 inch....................42.00

6 STEPS in MAKING a GOOD LAWN

above: The production and distribution of trade cards, catalogs, and other ephemera related to reel mowers and lawn care went into high gear when lawn mower production itself increased around 1880. Jim Ricci draws on this hard-to-find material to help him fill in the gaps in the history of the reel mower. *right:* Jim Ricci at home, practicing what he preaches.

functionality that he decided on the spot to investigate the field, research he calls that of an "industrial archaeologist." He also collects and preserves 19th- and early-20th-century horse and motor mowers, as well as catalogs, ephemera, literature, and photographs relating to the art and avocation of cutting grass (Ricci is not alone in his obsession—50 percent of Americans in a Gallup survey viewed their lawns as important to their self-esteem). Ricci hopes someday to create a museum dedicated to his chosen object of desire, although he admits it has been an uphill battle to convince some people of the worthiness of his quest.

"Somehow, it's okay to be serious about fishing rods or canoes," Jim observes, "but you have to explain lawn mowers, even to historians."

He doesn't have to explain them to gar-

"People know I'm interested, so sometimes they just drop them off," says Jim. "I add them to the collection."

Ricci's passion for reel mowers began in the early 1990s, when he first laid eyes upon a Locke reel mower, painted forest green with yellow pinstripes, with red dots at joints calling for regular applications of grease. The instrument struck him as such a felicitous combination of elegance and

deners, because the lawn is a kind of proletarian handmaiden to the garden, its lush greensward setting off what we tend to think of as the royal beauty of our annuals, perennials, and specimen trees and shrubs. Even if we take limited pleasure in the actual act of operating a lawn mower, we like the end result. It is the perfect frame for our horticultural picture.

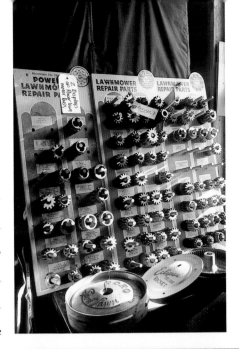

left: Repair shop displays of parts for ailing lawn mowers are stored temporarily in a room above Jim Ricci's garage; the collector hopes some day to create a museum devoted to reel mowers.

The lawn mower, like the lawn itself, was invented in England in the early 19th century, both being the consequences of the rise of a wealthy new leisure class spawned by the Industrial Revolution. Mowers came into their own in the United States in the years following the Civil War, when our own middle classes suddenly emerged with discretionary income and a yen, similar to that of their British cousins, for grassy yards and cottage gardens. Ricci guesses there were once between fifty and seventy-five reel mower manufacturers in the United States, serving this market. With the advent of power rotary mowers, first patented in the 1930s and common as crabgrass by the 1950s, once-respected names in lawn-maintenance machinery, such as Pennsylvania Lawnmower, FN Lawnmower, Coldwell, and Dille & McGuire, vanished from the face of the earth. One survivor, according to Ricci,

above: A few of the more than 500 reel mowers that Jim Ricci has amassed over the years.

has been the American Lawn Mower Co./ Great States Corp., founded in 1895 and still selling about 200,000 reel lawn mowers per year, presumably to fitness fanatics or people with postage-stamp lawns.

Times have changed, but today, to the gardener's ear, at any rate, something about the sound of a well-oiled, freshly sharpened reel mower is still vastly superior to the humdrum roar of its sit-down riding descendant.

Inspired Plantsmen, Passionate Collectors, and Singular Visions in the World of Gardening

below, left to right: Spring in the Hill Country of Texas brings a beehive of activity to many locales, none more so than the Antique Rose Emporium in Brenham, the Round Top Antiques Fair in Round Top, and the McAshan Herb Gardens at Festival Hill, also in Round Top.

EXCURSION: Texas Hill Country

When the first tufts of blue appear along the highways and back roads, Texans gear up for their favorite springtime spectator sport: wildflower watching.

—PATRICIA SHARPE, *Texas Monthly* (1997)

IN THE MIND'S EYE OF MOST TEXANS, THE HILL COUNTRY SURROUNDING THE

state capital of Austin is an idyllic place, where the sky is forever blue, the clouds are fleecy white, the land is bathed in sunlight, and the hills are carpeted with the purple-blue heads of bluebonnets.

Well, it's true in the spring . . . usually . . . depending on the weather. That's when wildflowers appear in great drifts across the rolling countryside, luring visitors by the thousands from city and suburb. Washington County, centered in Brenham, sponsors a photo contest every year, awarding a modest shopping certificate to the person who best captures the area's "slice of life." A few years ago the winning entry was a longhorn steer curled up in a field of bluebonnets.

There has been no better spokesperson for wildflower power as an aid to highway and roadside beautification than Texas's own Lady Bird Johnson. The National Wildflower Research Center, south of Austin, has been described as the former First Lady's "visionary gift to Texas." Founded by Lady Bird and actress Helen Hayes in 1982, the center has grown to become the nation's premier center for wildflower information and experimentation. Some five hundred species of native plants flourish in its ten-million-dollar botanical garden. With the largest rooftop rainwater-collection system in North America, the demonstration gardens and lawns at the center have survived the periodic droughts that afflict the Southwest. There is also a café, gift shop, and auditorium for lectures on the

grounds. Blending with traditional Hill Country farm buildings, all the structures in the compound are made of milky limestone and red sandstone.

Another pioneering lady, Emma Lee Turney of Houston, has made the town of Round Top, population eighty-one, and now many of the towns surrounding Round Top, synonymous with antiquing. More than three decades ago, she invited antiques dealers to set up shop for a long weekend in the spring in the town's historic Rifle Association Building, so-called for the marksmanship competitions that took place in its adjoining fields. "It was a marvelous country grange, with flaps ‹ let down on its sides for ventilation," Turney recalls upon seeing the building for the first time. "It had a freestanding peaked roof, and the high ceiling was hung with colorful red, white, and blue streamers, remnants of the latest Fourth of July celebration."

The event was such a hit that in following years it spread to other nearby venues. Now Emma Lee hosts her Round Top antiques and folk art fair twice a year, traditionally during the first full weekend in April and October. Dozens of other tented cities of Texana and Americana have since sprung up in the area to coincide with her fair, such as the Marburger Farm Antiques Fair, also in Round Top, the Warrenton Antiques Show and Sale, and the Shelby Antique Show. Gardeners are prominent among the collectors who flock to Round Top every year for all manner of gar-

below: As a writer in a 1941 issue of *Texas Parade* once declared, "springtime is when the sky falls on Texas." Brilliant patches of bluebonnets appear between March and May, along with many other wildflowers, notably Indian paintbrush and Drummond's phlox. The annual flowering prompts Texans and other visitors to head for the hills, cameras in hand.

below: Scenes from Emma Lee Turney's Round Top Antiques Fair, where garden ornaments and furnishings are never in short supply, and unique regional art such as bluebonnet paintings is snapped up by collectors, decorators, and designers. Now more than thirty years since its founding, the show brings in around 300 dedicated dealers of Americana from around the country, attracting thousands of collectors to the small central Texas town of Round Top.

dening paraphernalia—from tools to urns and birdbaths to gazebos, as well as art, books, and other materials suitable for furnishing an indoor garden room—all priced to sell.

Gardeners who shop Round Top should try to make room in their schedules for a visit to the delightful McAshan Herb Garden at Festival Hill, home of the renowned music institute founded by pianist James Dick. Madalene Hill is curator of the gardens and Gwen Barclay, her daughter, is director of food service for the institute. The two collaborated on *Southern Herb Growing,* first published in 1987 and now considered a classic on the subject of herbs and herbal cooking. The gardens they have created here include a cloister garden laid out amid simulated ruins and fashioned after the meditative space of a monastery, and a set of raised beds displaying herbal plants from around the world. The pair conduct tours, herbal seminars complete with tastings, and lectures at Festival Hill in the spring and fall, when the gardens are at their best.

Michael Shoup is another pioneering Texas gardener, whose Antique Rose Emporium, an eight-acre complex of "not rose gardens, but gardens with roses in them," as he says, can be found in nearby Brenham. The place has the friendly atmosphere of a botanical theme park, rather than a retail center, with its seductive walkways, red Radio Flyer wagons (for customers to haul their plants), a tractor-pulled train for kids, and a bottle tree—the product of an ancient African custom for trapping evil spirits, converted into a kind of yard art by descendants of slaves. On weekends there is even a barbecue stand, set up by members of a local church.

Although some folks come to the Antique Rose Emporium just for the fun of it (or to get married, in the chapel on the grounds), serious gardeners arrive to study how roses and other flowers have been incorporated into the display gardens, and to take home the high-quality plant materials, especially from among the more than three hundred varieties of antique varieties of rose shrubs and climbing rose vines, from Adam to Zephirine Drouhin, listed on the center's availability list.

"Modern roses are, essentially, exhibition roses—short-lived thoroughbreds of erect habit, demanding continuous pampering in order to contribute their overly brilliant perfect flowers," writes Shoup in his *Roses in the Southern Garden* (2000). "On the other hand, we found that old roses are fragrant and disease-resistant, and more important, they have a diversity of form that makes them useful as a landscape plant."

Years ago, after touring botanical gardens around the world, Michael decided he much preferred personal, iconoclastic gardens, such as "yards with bottle trees and tire planters, small water gardens crowded with horsetail and goldfish, a small border devoted to a color scheme of red or white, fruit trees bordered with parsley, fountains filled with marbles, and ornate vine-covered mailboxes." All these he found fascinating because "there were no rules, only a purposeful decision by someone to mix this with that and see what happened."

opposite, clockwise from top left: **Pioneering herbalist Madalene Hill is the curator of the McAshan Herb Gardens at Festival Hill in Round Top; she and her late husband, Jim, along with daughter Gwen Barclay, operated the renowned Hilltop Herb Farm in Cleveland, Texas, near Houston, for more than thirty years. Nasturtium, rosemary, and hundreds of other herbs grow in profusion at Festival Hill in the setting of a cloister built with native stone. Annie McClure of Shreveport, Lousiana, sets up shop for her business, Nest, in Round Top every year, catering to gardeners and collectors. McClure's offerings include naturalist collections, botanical specimens, rural furniture, architectural elements, and farm artifacts.**

below, left to right: The Antique Rose Emporium in Brenham, Texas, founded by G. Michael Shoup in 1983, is an all-purpose garden center with a special emphasis on old garden roses, offering more than 300 varieties. A bottle tree on the grounds evokes folklore dating back to glassblowers in 9th-century Africa, when tribes used glass objects as talismans against evil spirits; evolving into a form of yard art in this country, bottle trees have been called "the poor person's stained-glass window." Tommy Flowers, whose father, Henry, designs gardens at the Rose Emporium, takes a water break. Display gardens at the Antique Rose Emporium offer gardeners ideas for planting both climbing and shrub varieties of roses.

"ROSES of the WEEK"
1)FRAGRANCE: MAGGIE-PENELOPE
2)SHRUBS: CALDWELL PINK-LAMARNE
3) CLIMBERS: RED CASCADE-SOMBREUIL
4)LOW BORDERS: THE FAIRY
5)MID-SIZE BUSHES:
& MRS. R.M. FINCH

3
SINGULAR VISIONS

There is no such thing as a style fitted for every situation; only one who knows and studies the ground well will ever make the best of a garden, and any "style" may be right where the site fits it.

—WILLIAM ROBINSON, *The English Flower Garden* (1883)

Artists often bring their own quirky sensibilities to their garden spaces. The raw materials of space, color, volume, and shape are their building blocks in the garden, just as they are in their own art forms. They violate conventional aesthetic belief at various turns. If in their compulsion to be fresh and original they create outrageous departures from the norm—using a pyramid of colorful bowling balls, say, as a focal point (as visitors find at the entrance to the garden of collage-construction artist Johanna Nitke Marquis, on a hillside overlooking Puget Sound and the Olympia Mountains in Washington)—they challenge our preconceptions in a winning way.

Humor and surprise are endemic to the gardens of Marquis and eleven other artists featured in the book *Artists in Their Gardens* (2001), by Valerie Easton and David Laskin. The volume limits its scope to gardens in the benign maritime climate of the Pacific Northwest, but that region is such a cauldron of horticultural diversity and creativity that it still offers lessons for gardeners everywhere. And, like politics, all gardening is local, anyway.

"Passion is the key," write the authors in their introduction. "It's what artists have more of than ordinary mortals. The passion to take risks, go with their obsessions, and simply to be crazy because it's fun."

Thus sculptor Les Bugajski has carved gentle faces in stone and wood for various locations in his garden in Vancouver, Washington, "so that I'm never alone." Painter Grant Leier aggressively furnishes his garden on Vancouver Island with tag-sale knickknacks, hand-painted birdbaths, and gaudily painted animals cut out of sheet metal. "If you have driftwood," he says, "you should at least paint it bright orange to tart it up a bit. A garden without manipulation is really dull." And ceramic artist Anne Hirondelle has created "a hushed, calm, Zen-like oasis of a garden" on the Olympic Peninsula, characterized by subtly defined garden rooms devoid of bright colors and ostentatious forms, "a garden so full of serenity, that even a black Lab, that most rambunctious of dogs, would feel compelled to pause in his mad dash beneath the vine-draped entry pergola and put each paw down slowly and carefully as he soaked up the tranquillity."

opposite: Framed with shore juniper and Indian hawthorne, the bromeliads and succulents in the garden of a California artist provide a "red room" for visitors to contemplate.

Separate galls, showing pupa and imago

magnified 9-10 times

The singular visions of the artists and gardeners featured in *The Gardener's Life* may not be everybody's cup of tea, either, but their examples can't help but nudge the honest gardener into taking another look at his or her way of seeing things in the garden, at the degree of harmony and contrast found between site and style, in that garden, and perhaps to contemplate introducing some changes, radical or conservative, into the grand design for the next new growing season. As Easton and Laskin correctly remind us:

"Garden-making is a process,
one to be enjoyed with no
thought of completion."

clockwise from top left: Craftsmanship shapes the gardening vision in many forms, including a beautifully thrown terra-cotta pot, a replica of a plant in painted glass, and a topiary-like rendering of a carnation in a hand-colored plate dated 1731.

The Aerial View

It is wonderful how much work one can find to do in so tiny a plot of land.

—CELIA THAXTER, *An Island Garden Daybook* (1894)

"I see horticulture through the eyes of an artist, not the lens of a botanist," notes Abbie Zabar in her book *A Growing Gardener* (1996), a unique personal expression of an urbanite's love affair with plants. Filled with the author's own delightful drawings and calligraphy, the volume describes what it is like to garden "21 stories above asphalt and cement," and is a fitting tribute to the magical landscape Abbie created in the heart of New York City over a period of two decades.

"Conditions are exaggerated at this height," she says. "It is ten times more windy, or sunny, or hot here than at street level. If you forget to water at ground level, roots go deeper into the soil. If you forget to water here, you get a dead plant."

Among "the real estate of architectural air," in the poet Howard Moss's phrase, the view from Abbie's penthouse apartment encompasses the green expanse of Central Park, a monument called *Cleopatra's Needle* in the foreground. "The way I look at it," she says, "I'm just borrowing some bushes from the yard across the street that's more than two miles long." Facing north, away from the park, the George Washington Bridge spans the Hudson River. The tumultuous cityscape all around somehow fades when one is on the terrace proper, such is the calming effect of its design. Twenty-five running feet of yew hedge and a row of twelve-foot-high European hornbeams,

opposite, from left to right: Agave parryi, an outsider art composite of concrete and wire from France, and *Scirpus cernuus*, also known as fiberoptic grass, echo the skyline along New York's Central Park. Although damaged, the clay pot was decoratively restored with wire.

above: Diminutive tools are best suited for cultivating and weeding Abbie Zabar's many miniature gardens. Her cat Milly was found as a stray in Brooklyn.
above right: A pot of lavender 'Hidcote' has been underplanted with wooly thyme, with what Abbie calls her "Central Park rock collection" used as mulch.

pruned as a green screen, provide an elegant backdrop for facing teak benches, the gift of a friend, modeled after Abbie's favorite bench, found in the gardens at Sissinghurst in England.

Speaking of Sissinghurst, Abbie, who in the summer months is in the garden when it is coolest, in both morning and night, recalls faxing the world-renowned garden with a question on training hop vines, an exhibit of which she had seen there, but not paid attention to, on a visit

in 1999. "I was asking, but felt more like I was begging, for any information on the hops exhibit," she relates. "And suddenly at five A.M. on a June day in New York, I'm out watering and my phone is ringing. 'Good morning, Sissinghurst Castle calling. Is it too early for you?'" She says she was so excited it might as well have been Buckingham Palace on the other end.

"Beautiful gardens must be ethereal yet grounded, flexible yet resilient," declares Zabar, so while spiral arborvitae lend elegance to her perch on Manhattan, there are also flowering chives for salads and catnip for the cats, Milly and Willy. And there are Russian sage plants, lavender

me of my cats," she says. "Willy and Milly like a cozy place to curl up, but they also need room to stretch." Abbie collects tiny antique books no more than 4 inches high, which she has rebound in library cloth, and she herself is something of a miniatur-

aplenty, and vines of morning glory and clematis. Bees and fireflies buzz the place in the summer. In fall birds feed on the reddish hawthorn berries and purple-berried clusters of Boston ivy vine. "To garden is to share" is another of Abbie's mantras, and so life is eventful here, with visits from mockingbirds, sparrows, and even monarch butterflies. Every year, a pair of red-tailed hawks build their nest in a limestone pediment a few buildings over, and she has the pleasure of watching them soar by her windows all spring.

The challenge of high-rise gardening has made Abbie an expert on planting in containers. "Plants that live in pots remind

clockwise from above:
Varieties of *Semper-vivum,* known popularly as hens-and-chicks, along with *Lithops,* or flowering-stone plant, lend an otherworldly aspect to an urban garden. A tiny match strike is planted with *Sempervivum* 'King Charles'. Children's tools were given handles fashioned out of wisteria vines by Maryland artist Bobby Hansson.

ist. In fact one of the books, an essay on the poetic imagination by Carl Zigrosser, is titled *Multum in Parvo*—"much in little"—and that is an apt description for her collection of crevice-loving alpine plants in antique troughs and chipped and chiseled granite pavers; for her stone urns, overflowing with countless varieties of sempervivums (of which she sometimes feels she holds "The National Collection," as they would say in England); for her strawberry

pot, also planted with hens and chickens as well as a tiny variety of aquilegia; and, in a minuscule match strike nearby, a cluster of lithops, African plants that mimic the appearance of stones to fool desert predators. Not to mention her favorite garden tools, fashioned from children's implements and so ideal for small plant surgeries. The handles were carved for her out of wisteria and other vines by another friend, Maryland artist Bobby Hansson.

Similarly, as an artist, Abbie thrives in small spaces. In an ongoing project of now ten years' duration, she is documenting the famous flower arrangements in the Great Hall of the Metropolitan Museum, which are changed weekly (out of funds left as a bequest by *Reader's Digest* cofounder Lila Acheson Wallace for that purpose). She translates the spectacular arrangements into intimately scaled colored-pencil drawings on cardboard, without however sacrificing their monumental quality.

"I wasn't interested in reproducing a botanical exactness," the artist recalls. "To create the illusion of these dramatic bouquets—that's what intrigues me," an artistic feat called "classical illusion."

In the spring of 2000, when the drawings were the subject of a show sponsored by the Horticultural Society of New York, Abbie observed that capturing the weekly changing floral bouquets in the early morning light and limited time she had available, during the hour and a half before the museum opened its doors, meant that her working drawings were always her final impressions.

"A long time ago I was a staff artist for a daily newspaper," she explains. "I got used to drawing on location and even to the rush. There was no waiting for a muse to hit when the production department was throwing deadlines at you. I swear it was the best art school I ever went to." She adds, "Maybe if I have more time, more light—even just some room to spread out with my pencils—life might be too comfortable to draw."

above left: The textural quality of Abbie Zabar's plant compositions comes as much from the containers she chooses as from the plants themselves, in this case *Saxifraga cotyledon* var. *pyramidalis. above:* One of many colored-pencil drawings on cardboard that the artist has made of the flower arrangements in the Great Hall of the Metropolitan Museum of Art. *overleaf:* A row of European hornbeams (*Carpinus betulus* 'Fastigiata') and a yew hedge (*Taxus* 'Brownii') form the backdrop for a spectacular terrace garden twenty-one stories off the ground. Milly, one of Abbie's two cats, seems at home in the tranquil setting with a terra-cotta rabbit and a stone squirrel.

The artist's striking works have appeared, either as exhibits or as parts of permanent collections, in the Louvre, the Smithsonian Institution, and the Hunt Institute for Botanical Documentation in Pittsburgh. Her studio, adjoining the terrace, has a collection of old clay pots, a peg rack hanging with antique tools, and a poster for her first book, *The Potted Herb,* which earned the 1989 Award of Excellence from the Garden Writers of America. Stairs lead down to her apartment, sparely furnished, visually stunning, with collections of Shaker baskets and early-20th-century English trugs, and art at every turn, even on pillows and bed linens bearing what has become a kind of domestic logo—a minuscule image of an evergreen tree, complete with root ball, in cross-stitch.

Although everything in Abbie's office, home, and garden appears deployed with a perfectionist's zeal, the artist has learned from experience that no garden is without fault or failure, and that patience, flexibility, and compromise are the gardener's necessary virtues.

"I'm not like the people who want every blade of grass to be perfect," she says. "Gardening is a combination of design and horticulture, but it is a fugitive art; it comes and goes."

clockwise from left: Collections of early-20th-century trugs and Shaker baskets, the latter made by Martha Wetherbee from original Shaker molds, lend their minimalist charm to the bedroom. Willy rests by a pillow bearing Abbie's unofficial logo, an evergreen tree with a root ball. Drawings in the Great Hall series inform the living room with the idea of "horti-culture through the eyes of an artist, not the lens of a botanist."

A Californian's Shangri-La

May your flowers flourish, your bees prosper, your birds love you, and your pet fishes live forever.

—SHIRLEY HIBBARD, *Rustic Adornments for Homes of Taste* (1856)

In the foothills of Santa Barbara, a pair of large, rustic wooden gates swing open upon a journey, for the first-time visitor, that is certain to surprise, to captivate, and, finally, to utterly seduce.

From the gate, a 1,000-foot drive drops through a lush, green tropical setting, then veers off and brings one in front of a Caribbean-style plantation house, surrounded by palm trees, with a red tin roof, shuttered windows, and a wraparound porch where hummingbirds flock to feeders with manic intensity, while Susie, a blue weimaraner, dozes by the door.

And that is only the beginning. Below the house, an English perennial garden follows the lines of a meandering creek that feeds into three connecting ponds, passing by old sheds faded to a yellow-green patina. A bridge invites the visitor to cross this creek in the direction of a beckoning set of stone steps that itself leads up and into an expansive Victorian rose garden with Oriental touches, its arbors thickly laden with pink and white blooms, and its pergola covered with Chinese white and purple wisteria, overlooking a pond afloat with lotuses and tropical water lilies.

And there is more. Walk through the garden to the other side and enter a tunnel of pendulous *Datura*—angel's trumpets—giant birds of paradise, banana trees,

opposite: Evoking a life of luxury in the Caribbean, this plantation-style house in the foothills of Santa Barbara, with its generous porches lined with potted azalea topiaries and shuttered windows, is only one of many surprises awaiting visitors to the home and gardens of Bobby Webb.

and more palms of numerous varieties, all underplanted in a sea of fern. Here is, of all things, a range of beautifully crafted, spacious avaries housing brilliantly colored toucans and parrots, African and Asian

clockwise from above:

clockwise from above: Lotuses and tropical water lilies grow in a pond at one end of the formal rose garden, with canna lilies bordering the water and Chinese white and purple wisteria climbing the elegantly designed pergola. Bobby Webb (right) and Michael Corbett with their parrot, one of their many exotic birds. Besides aviaries, Bobby has built a 40-foot-high enclosure, complete with cascading ponds, for his flamingos.

hornbills, cranes, ostriches, emus, rheas, and other exotic birds. The pièce de résistance: a spectacular flock of flamingos within a 140-by-70-foot habitat, 40 feet high, with two cascading ponds and an elevated walkway.

Welcome to the home of Bobby Webb and Michael Corbett, located in a secluded bowl of land surrounded by steep rises of dense vegetation, with a huge expanse of blue sky overhead. Only a few minutes

from downtown Santa Barbara, it feels uncannily remote, a modern-day Shangri-la full of living things, and bristling with life.

Bobby Webb is in the business of creating one-of-a-kind estates, complete with elaborate gardens, so it was no surprise he would pull out all stops when it came time to build the home he shares with Michael. Strikingly original for its California setting, part of the inspiration for the original design came from the old tin-roofed buildings that Webb had found on the property when he bought it, and part came from a Hollywood movie set he had once seen that re-created the look of a house in Havana, Cuba. "It had a certain flair that I liked," he recalls, so from that point he began fleshing out details for the house and its interiors, by poring over books and photographs that captured the Caribbean building style. His brother, Joseph, made the actual drawings for the final design.

Bobby's passion for birds and gardens has its roots in a storybook childhood. "My father, Richard Webb, supplied animals for the movies," he explains. "I spent my summers on movie sets for films like *Ben-Hur, El Cid, Cimarron,* and *Giant.* People like John Wayne and Robert Taylor were just folks—friends of my dad—to me. Through him I met trainers who worked with exotic birds, and that's how I became fascinated by them. I've had birds ever since."

Starting with pigeons and chickens as a boy, Bobby soon advanced to breeding parakeets and canaries. The time-lapse photography of canaries hatching in the movie *Birdman of Alcatraz,* starring Burt Lancaster, featured eggs borrowed from the youngster's collection.

For a time the family lived on a fifteen-acre property in Pacific Palisades owned by an avid gardener named Winifred Knowlton. "I basically grew up gardening at Winnie's side," Webb recalls. "She was a mentor to me, sharing her knowledge of plants, showing me how to make cuttings, nurturing further my already strong interest in gardening. I had my own vegetable garden when I was ten." One Christmas his parents, aware of his interest in growing orchids and other exotic plants, presented him with a small greenhouse. "They were always surprising us with unusual gifts—homing pigeons, for example, or a rare kind of peacock."

below: Having planted thousands of roses, both disease-resistant climbing roses and hybrid tea roses, the owners have enough cut flowers to fill every room in the house from March through November, including a dining room with English tables and chairs.

right: A guest bedroom in the highest reaches of the house has windows looking out on all sides. *below:* The pool housing Bobby Webb's collection of koi fish features a sandstone sculpture of an Indian royal family that Michael Corbett discovered in an importer's Los Angeles showroom; water spouts spill into the pool, which features cattails and papyrus grass grown in pots. When they surface for feeding, the koi fish provide a dazzling display of color and motion.

Fragile Beauties

Flowers have such a spontaneous appeal that it is sometimes hard to remember that nature produces them for a practical purpose and not just to give us pleasure.

—DENISE OTIS, *Decorating with Flowers* (1978)

For decades, the most popular exhibit, hands down, at the Harvard Museum of Natural History in Cambridge, Massachusetts, has been the Ware Collection of Blaschka Glass Models of Plants, known simply as "the glass flowers." Created expressly for the university by Leopold and Rudolf Blaschka, a father-and-son team of glass artisans in Germany, between 1887 and 1936, the more than 3,000 ingeniously crafted models represent more than 830 species of plants, ranging from the ethereally beautiful fleur-de-lis iris to the pendulously threatening carnivorous pitcher plant of Malaya.

With images rendered faithfully from nature and anatomical sections of various floral and vegetative parts of the plants, the models were originally commissioned as teaching tools and they are still used as such by students in plant sciences at Harvard. But tourists, plant lovers, garden clubs, and schoolchildren constitute the vast majority of the more than 100,000 visitors who take time to "smell" the glass flowers every year.

Obsessive and secretive, the Blaschkas were rumored to have invented unusual

opposite: In contrast to real plants, which flower for only a short period of time, Harvard's glass flowers are in bloom all year round and consequently make superb teaching tools.

Transverse section of ovary
magnified 36 times

Style
magnified 36 times

Stamens
magnified 36 times

Fruits

first made a rough sketch of the relations of all the flowers to each other and to the leaves, and then mixed glass with colors to get the right tints. The corolla was drawn and formed from a tube of glass. Then the petals were formed and melted to the tube of the corolla. The stamens were melted in next, and then the whole thing was placed in an annealing oven, where it remained for a few hours. It took an hour and a half to make the tubes and petals of three Phlox flowers. It required about an hour to put in the stamens and add the calyx. Next, the buds were fastened to wires covered with glass. All of these were next fastened to a stem with leaves and the model was then ready for paint.

clockwise from above:
One of the cherrywood cabinets in which the glass flowers are displayed. A 1940 volume on the collection called the father-son team who created the flowers "not only workers in glass but naturalists as well, so that their models are a combination of artistic ability and scientific interpretation." An exhibit of the maple family includes *Acer rubrum*, red maple.

techniques to create their models, a notion they ridiculed. "Many people think that we have some secret apparatus by which we can squeeze glass suddenly into these forms," Leopold once stated, "but it is not so. We have tact. My son Rudolf has more than I have, because he is my son, and tact increases in every generation."

Dr. George Lincoln Goodale, the botanical museum's first director, witnessed the Blaschkas at work and once described the process of flower-making in a letter to Elizabeth C. and Mary Lee Ware (who funded the project). Basically, the brothers

Welcome as they are, at least in principle, the unbridled enthusiasm of schoolchildren—their hands oblivious to the DO NOT TOUCH signs posted, and their tramping feet sending vibrations like jackhammers through the cherrywood display cases housing the fragile exhibits—makes curators cringe. Damage has occurred over the years, in the form of fissures on this leaf or that blossom and faded colors and delaminations.

"People will come and say, 'Oh, the glass flowers are magnificent,' and they are," says Susan Rossi-Wilcox, who began volunteering at the museum more than two decades ago and now serves as administrator and curatorial protector. "But in the back of my mind I'm thinking about the extensive repairs that are needed."

Meanwhile, just like a magician with his smoke and mirrors, the glass flowers of the Blaschkas continue, tactfully, to deceive and delight.

Cat Crossing Farm

It was with flowers that the grandmothers bound the folk together, and with flowers that they trained the children.

—E. P. POWELL, *Grandmother's Garden* (1915)

Doug Jimerson knew he had found home the moment he turned into the driveway of a tiny, two-story, four-square house in the middle of a cornfield in Iowa. "It had the same design sensibilities as the place where I grew up in New Jersey," he recalls, "with the same old roses and old arbors that my grandmother had loved." He remembers saying to himself as he pulled to a stop, "This is Nana's yard."

He was twenty-five at the time, several years out of Iowa State University, with three strikes against him as a potential tenant: "I'd been looking for a place to rent for a year and a half, but I was single, male, and had pets; finally, I decided to buy."

If his preliminary impression of the hundred-year-old farmhouse, thirty miles northwest of Des Moines, was favorable, his reaction when he walked into the garage on the property, which was filled to eye level with piles of stuff, was on the scale of a revelation from on high.

"On one of the walls was a cover of *Better Homes & Gardens,* the magazine my grandmother had long subscribed to, from the issue of November 1951, which is the month and year I was born," he says, "and stapled next to it was a picture of a collie, which was one of the animals I owned at the time. I just knew I was meant to live in this place."

opposite: A dozen or so cats have the run of the place at the Iowa farmstead of Karen and Doug Jimerson, but the sheep and other animals are confined to the back pasture. The old gate, school bell, and various other garden ornaments were found at auctions and flea markets.

Two decades later, Doug and his wife, Karen Weir-Jimerson, a certified master gardener in her own right, had completely transformed the property without, however, losing touch with the gardening sensibility that had intrigued Doug in the first place. Doubling the size of the house provided more room to display collections of garden books, old seed boxes, floral oil paintings, prints of sheepdogs in action, among many other things. Not incidentally, it also gave their teenage sons, Tristan and Graham, more of the growing room they needed.

The couple named the place Cat Crossing Farm after an incident that occurred years before when Doug was still single and sharing an apartment with a friend, photographer Pete Krumhardt, and several cats, on a busy street in Ames, Iowa.

Worried about the effect of traffic on their cats' safety, they put up a sign by the road that said CAT CROSSING (this long before precious versions of such signs became common in the garden marketplace). Town officials objected to the sign. Doug remembers making an impassioned defense of the sign at a city council meeting, which fell on disbelieving if not deaf ears.

Six distinctive garden areas have been staked out on today's Cat Crossing Farm. A perennial border is planted in front of the house, along a 95-foot iron fence that Karen found in Texas and hauled back to Iowa in sections. The other gardens that have been created over the years each measure 60 by 40 feet. A cottage garden stands in front of an outbuilding that has served both as a work studio and guest house, most recently improved with the

addition of a hot tub. Across from it stands a raised, formal garden. Then there is the shade garden, with a long, meandering path under the trees with tens of thousands of spring bulbs, in the middle of which is found a large aviary housing a dozen white ringneck doves, and the meadow garden, a hillside location packed with native prairie wildflowers.

Finally, there is the garden known as Provence, because it is planted with rosemary, lavender, and other aromatic herbs and flowers of the Mediterranean. It contains a water feature and a romantic sitting area under an arbor covered with grapes and moonflower vine. In late summer, when the acres of corn directly behind the garden have tasseled out at 12 to 15 feet

high, Provence becomes as fine and private a place as that preeminent chronicler of the south of France, Peter Mayles himself, could imagine.

The Jimersons' cats and dogs have pretty much free rein in all the garden areas, but horses, sheep, and donkeys are confined to a back pasture. The couple's latest four-legged acquisitions are Ben and Sam, stocky Haflinger draft ponies to be used to pull carts and, when there is snow on the ground, to pull an antique sleigh that Karen bought at auction. After grow-

clockwise from top left: Karen with her quarter horse, Yukon. The Mediterranean garden known as Provence is a congenial setting for entertaining when the corn is as high as an elephant's eye. A pair of donkeys, part of the extensive menagerie at Cat Crossing Farm. *overleaf:* Folk art captures the essence of country life inside and outside the Jimerson homestead.

above: An old farmstand sign graces the back porch, along with a collection of laboratory vials recycled as bud vases. The orchid sits in a large stoneware crock inscribed with the name of the farm.

When Doug became gardening editor of Meredith Corporation's *Better Homes & Gardens* some years ago, it was as if he had come full circle. In fact, the formal garden behind the house was originally the location of the magazine's first test garden, where new plant varieties were tried out and editorial features were produced.

"As a kid I remember the magazine coming to my grandmother every month," Doug recalls, "but when an issue didn't have a garden story in it, I would throw it across the room." His intimate knowledge of all the garden stories that had been published by the magazine in the 1960s and 1970s, which he had devoured as a child, was an obvious asset on the job. More recently he has been the head of Meredith's special-interest garden magazines, producing a staggering three thousand pages of garden editorial matter a year for ten titles and a total of twenty-three issues, none of which get thrown across the room anymore. For her part, Karen has written and edited four garden books and was editorial director of the late lamented website Garden.com.

Better Homes & Gardens, by the way, has always had its roots firmly in the heartland. Before it came into being, the enterprising Edwin T. Meredith had launched,

ing up in West Des Moines, Karen went to the University of Iowa in Iowa City. Before meeting Doug, through a mutual friend, she obtained a master's degree in English at the University of South Carolina, producing a collection of poetry under the supervision of her thesis advisor, the poet and novelist James Dickey.

Both Doug and Karen have been involved in garden magazine and book publishing for most of their working lives.

in October 1902, the first issue of *Success-ful Farming,* aimed at the pragmatic farmers of the Corn Belt. At this time, with the advent of power tractors and hybridization, the volume and value of American

left: A jumble of rustic birdhouses on the front porch bears a distinct midwestern provenance.

farm products had increased from a yearly average of $703 million to $1.9 billion. With the success of his farming magazine (still going strong today), Meredith cast about for something that would appeal to a nonfarm audience, and came up with

Fruit, Garden and Home. The first issue appeared in July 1922, with a cover price of ten cents. The magazine morphed into *Better Homes & Gardens* in 1924 and eventually grew to become a perennial leader in the women's service field.

above: The studio–guest house is filled with gardening paraphernalia, including old watering cans and glass cloches.

Inspired Plantsmen, Passionate Collectors, and Singular Visions in the World of Gardening

left: An old blue-painted pie safe in the dining room is surrounded by images of sheepherding.

above: A ceramic border collie in full working stance, next to a collection of old gardening books. *left:* A seed sampler, originally a teaching tool, was a present to Doug from a friend.

Doug Jimerson's singular vision for Cat Crossing Farm derives from a passion that came into being at an early age, nurtured by a grandmother who trusted him to water her house plants and prune her roses. Not that everything always went smoothly between them. His penchant for raising large numbers of rabbits, frogs, and box turtles in the tiny yard sometimes ran at cross-purposes to her plans. "Nana especially disliked my box turtles, because they would tunnel under her rosebushes," Doug recalls. "She'd upend them by turning the garden hose on them, and I'd have to go out and rescue them."

But by and large Frances Dakin, who died in 1977, had an extraordinarily positive impact on the boy. At the age of seven, with her help, he ordered his first zonal geraniums through the mail. He read his grandmother's dog-eared copy of *The Wise Garden Encyclopedia* from cover to cover when he was twelve. He remembers taking the train with her to visit an azalea grower on Long Island, and coming back cradling young plants on their laps. When his folks bought a home in Mystic Islands, New Jersey, he landscaped the whole place for them, including planting his first vegetable garden, complete with looseleaf lettuces no one in the neighborhood had ever tasted

before, which came to be known as "Doug's lettuces." He was in eighth grade at the time.

"Basically, I grew up wanting to grow up on a farm," he says. "I think I ordered every farm set ever offered by the Sears catalog." The gardening gene having skipped a generation, Doug's own parents had no interest in the subject. "I remember frequent trips when my dad would speed by this lily pond center in New Jersey, a place I was dying to visit"—this at a time when Doug was drawing imaginary water gardens, amply populated with turtles and frogs, on paper. Many years later, working as a garden editor, Jimerson finally got to pull over and check out the place.

Ball pitchers, made in Ohio by the Hall company in the 1930s, are a colorful addition in the kitchen. The small dish in the plate rack is a memento of an early Iowa State Fair.

View Finder

Beginning at least as early as hieroglyphic flower illustration, the artist's interests were not necessarily in the appearance of a flower seen from a certain viewpoint, but in conveying the idea of a flower.

—SMITH COLLEGE MUSEUM OF ART EXHIBITION CATALOG, *Orchids and Artists, Five Centuries of Botanical Illustration* (1991)

opposite: Photographer Judith McMillan's standard equipment is her Zone 6 4 by 5-inch large format camera, but she has also obtained remarkable images of plants and insects using an X-ray machine from the Cleveland Museum of Natural History.

The house in a semirural setting east of Cleveland started thirty-five years ago as a small cottage in an overgrown apple orchard. The more that Judith and Ted McMillan added gardens to the landscape, the harder it became to leave for greener, bigger pastures, so two children, five house additions, and a Herculean water-garden project later, the McMillans are still in place, and happily so. The house still buzzes with life even though the children have gone out on their own, and is filled with examples of Judith's passion for gardening, none more enticing than her unique X-rayed botanicals.

"The gladioli, water lilies, tulips, orchids, columbine, and magnolia that are among her subjects take on a strangely translucent life, as though we are seeing but not seeing the objects," wrote art critic Laurie Schreiber in a review of a recent exhibition of McMillan's work in Maine, where the family has a summer house. "The spidery veins of a maple leaf, the multiple petticoats of a flower's petals are like ghostly layers resting lightly on each other, as our view, failing to come to its expected rest on the surface

clockwise from above:
The banks of Judith and Ted McMillan's water garden are planted with hostas, Shasta daisies, irises, daylilies, goatsbeard, and many other varieties. Above the orchid stand is one of the photographer's "optic explorations" of plant material using an X-ray machine. Judith's self-portrait in scrap iron, depicting the artist as gardener; creating the shadow piece inadvertently led her into becoming a photographer.

of things, falls endlessly through the inner makings of the flora and insects the photographer chooses to reveal."

The most recent addition, a room with a wall of windows looking out on a lawn edged with hemlocks, rhododendron, and other blooming shrubs and trees, features a 20-foot-long interior wall with a mural, filled with natural plant and animal beauties, painted for the McMillans by Cleveland artist Jerry Arnold, "so that we have something to look at on a cloudy day," Judith says.

The mural was not painted strictly from Nature, featuring, as it does, an example of early spring's lady slipper orchid growing alongside summer's late-flowering Queen Anne's lace. The quail in the foreground does not even represent the bobwhite species found in Ohio. "It's a blue-feathered California quail," Judith laughs, "just because Jerry insisted on getting something blue into the picture."

A whimsical mural was just what the new garden room needed, but when it comes to McMillan's own art, stern fidelity to detail is paramount. Judith was primarily interested in metal work, not photography, when she enrolled in the Cleveland Institute of Art. An introductory design project, a shadow piece for her own yard, was the first art that she did that really related to the garden, as well as to her fascination with the folklore about the importance of a person's shadow. The self-portrait in scrap iron that stands in the middle of her lawn today depicts the artist holding a trowel and a cultivator. "After creating it, I had to photograph it to show how the shadow moved and changed," she recalls, "and that led me to the discovery of photography. I took a photography class so I could document my work better, but once in the class, the love for photography took over."

McMillan was so enthralled with the new medium that she acquired the landscape photographer's dream apparatus, a Zone 6 4 by 5-inch large format camera, and began documenting the natural world around her on hand-coated, individually exposed platinum prints. Twenty square inches of negative is a huge canvas for a photographer to work in, affording possibilities for nuance and detail not readily available in other formats. "It produces the most archival image there is," she observes,

"one that is embedded in the paper itself, not on the surface."

With her artist's eye, Judith saw beauty in the unremarkable: a carpet of apples dropped in an abandoned orchard, or a wild marsh by a country road, teeming with amphibian and insect life, "vignettes," as she says, "that most people tend not to notice." Indeed, "Unnoticed Landscapes" became the title of two one-person exhibitions in Ohio that garnered much praise and several awards for her early work.

above: The elaborate water garden was made possible after the McMillans discovered their house was sitting on an aquifer.
overleaf: Judith McMillan's X-ray photograms have been acclaimed as "new and exciting, allowing the viewer to enter a world that is simultaneously spectral and highly technological."

Sull Life ck.
Optic Explorations

Meanwhile, McMillan had worked for years as a volunteer in the education department of the Cleveland Museum of Natural History, giving talks on Native Americans and wildlife indigenous to northeastern Ohio. Having become entranced with the visual properties of the objects and specimens in the museum's collection, however, she "decided on an art career rather than science when I went back to school," she relates, "and for my thesis project, I went back to the museum and photographed in the research collections to see how my trained eye would interpret the material."

One day, the curator of physical anthropology at the museum invited her to try his department's X-ray machine as another way of examining things, and when she saw examples he had played with, including images of shell, fish, and flower, she accepted, "and the big project was born.

"I concentrated almost exclusively on this project for four years," she continues. "It took many experiments to determine the level of radiation and length of radiation burn that would produce an X-ray that could function as a photographic negative. The exposure range that a doctor or

Judith K McMillan, 1992   Unnoticed Landscape #8-7

scientist would use to examine skeletal material creates a negative far too dense for printing as a photograph, and the normal levels of radiation burn through delicate plant material."

Once she mastered the technical obstacles, she began producing what amounts to X-ray photograms, describing the process thus: "I place my plant material directly on the loaded packet of X-ray film and then make the exposure. Everything I work with must fit on an eight-by-ten-inch sheet of film, and nothing can extend beyond the edges because the unit is enclosed like an oven.

"It's a challenge to create compositions that don't feel repetitive," she adds, "given the strict limitations. It's also difficult to

judge how layered material will look when X-rayed. Not only can my eye not see through the layers of material, I can't always determine how the variety of material is going to register on the film. But each and every limitation is a challenge which adds to the artistic progress."

As Laurie Schreiber sums up McMillan's achievement, "The result is new and exciting, allowing the viewer to enter a world that is simultaneously spectral and highly technological. What a pair of calla lilies or a collage of magnolia and a moth lose in hue—the images are black and white—they gain in the revelation of their inner texture."

Long before venturing into her experiments with the X-ray machine at the

above: Using her large-format camera, McMillan made this platinum print of a roadside marsh in 1992, one of a series she called "Unnoticed Landscapes."

above: Several varieties of hardy and tropical water lilies as well as lotuses grow in the water garden. The pond is also stocked with foot-long golden orfe, an ornamental fish originally from northern Eurasia.

the project quickly became one of the most expensive basements anyone ever built."

The contractor had to dig 280 feet around the house—all at below-basement level; the finished trench was 12 feet wide and 12 feet deep.

"It looked like we were building a free-way interchange," Judith recalls ruefully, and three beautiful apple trees they had managed to preserve from the original orchard had to be sacrificed. Watching them pulled up by the massive earthmoving equipment, "just like toothpicks coming out of hors d'oeuvres," brought her to tears, but, as she noted, "out of bad comes good.

"With running water now diverted to the ravine in our yard," she explained, "we used the dirt from the foundation to build a dam and create a water garden, complete with waterfall, where before we had just a damp ravine bottom with a shallow 'frog pond.'" Over the next few years, the pond was enlarged, including the addition of a second waterfall, lined, and planted with masses of spring- and summer-flowering astilbe, hosta, Siberian and Japanese iris, daylilies, acanthus, goatsbeard, and Japa-nese candelabra primroses. In the pond itself are several varieties of hardy and trop-ical water lilies as well as lotuses, which Judith herself periodically deadheads,

Natural History Museum, Judith set about to create a basement darkroom in her home, a decision that had profound and unexpected consequences for her amateur gardening career.

"Once excavation under the house began, we suddenly found out why there had never been much of a basement here in the first place," she explains. "We were located directly over an aquifer. The exist-ing foundation was sinking, the hole filling with water. Engineers were brought in, and

strapping on waist-high waders to do so.

"A weedy pest called string algae became a new problem in the pond, but through the Internet I discovered a solution using barley straw, which releases small amounts of hydrogen peroxide into

left and below: Amid flowering astilbe at water's edge, contented frogs, whom Judith McMillan jokingly likens to herself and her husband, Ted, take in the beautiful surroundings.

the water, controlling the algae," she explains. "It is wonderful to find a totally natural solution that works."

Now that her pond is clear, however, she has a new problem: A great blue heron, fishing here with great regularity, has apparently poked a hole in the pond liner as it jabs for fish. "We are trying to find the leak," she says, philosophically, "but the garden thrives and the fish are happy. Besides, for a gardener, what is a garden but a challenge?"

Orchids and the City

Being an orchid hunter has always meant pursuing beautiful things in terrible places.

—SUSAN ORLEAN, *The Orchid Thief* (1998)

opposite: Designer Vicente Wolf keeps his orchids on an 18th-century Italian console in the bedroom because he likes "to wake up with the blooms." The orchids come from as far away as Hawaii and as close as New York's flower market.

Whenever the frenetic lifestyle of a successful Manhattan professional threatens to get to him, interior designer and photographer Vicente Wolf turns to his orchids to lift his spirits.

"The orchids always bring life and a sense of surprise and awe," says the Cuban-born author of the recently published *Learning to See: Bringing the World Around You into Your Home* (2002), a book superficially about decorating and collecting but also a kind of manual for learning to look at one's environment in fresh new ways.

In the environment of Wolf's own loft, in a gritty neighborhood of parking garages and bus terminals just west of the Garment District, dozens of orchids in varying stages of bloom not only soothe the soul but accent a stunning collection of 20th-century photographs by the likes of Eugène Atget, Edward Weston, Edward Steichen, Richard Avedon, and Diane Arbus, as well as numerous artifacts and objets d'art found in the course of his extensive travels in Europe and Asia. "There aren't that many things that can bring me that much pleasure," Wolf says of the orchids. He makes sure he always has enough orchids in the loft to ensure that at least several of them will be in bloom at any given time. "They are like children. You take care of them and visually they take care of you."

above: Photographs in Wolf's extensive collection are propped up everywhere in his loft apartment, to encourage visitors to pick them up for a closer look. The finger "self-portrait" is by John Coplans.

their ornate frames." He pored over the photographs in old copies of *National Geographic,* whetting an appetite for travel to exotic places that continues to this day.

Wolf's parents were importers of building materials, and many of their friends were architects. For the young Vicente, "construction sites became as familiar to me as playgrounds were to most other children," he recalls. "I was aware of floor plans and used to draw them out for myself, imagining spaces in my mind. In the loneliness caused by my disability, I dwelled in my own little world, arranging things, making order." Once, when his parents bought a new house, the furniture arrived just when they were leaving for work. By the time they came home, the youngster had arranged the furniture in every room.

When Vicente (who today patiently answers to "Vincent" as well) came to New York, after the family had left Cuba for Miami in 1961, he tried his hand at various jobs, including acting, "which was utterly hopeless because I couldn't memorize lines." A chance meeting with his future design partner, Bob Patino, who was then working in a showroom for a fabric house, revealed a new career path and he got a job working with interior designers.

Growing up with an undiagnosed case of dyslexia in Havana in the 1950s, Wolf struggled so much with reading and other subjects at school that he became something of a loner, a path that would inadvertently enrich and strengthen the visual sensibility that he draws upon today in his work. He spent countless hours wandering through the Museum of Modern Art in Havana, "finding solace in the colors and composition of the paintings," as he writes in the introduction to his book, "and admiring

"By a stroke of luck, I had circled back to an old pastime from my childhood—planning interiors and doing drawings," he says, and it was only a matter of time before he would finally find his niche. "One day I was sweeping floors in a showroom," he recalls. "A year later my first decorating job appeared in *House Beautiful.*"

Wolf planted and maintains the wisteria on his New York terrace, nurtures all his orchids, and planted all the new greenery at his house in Montauk, Long Island. He has a design aesthetic that responds to gardens. "I remember sitting for hours in a garden in Kyoto, Japan," he relates, "just trying to see what the garden had to say. I like the Oriental point of view that gardens are for meditation and to help people recharge themselves spiritually. In the typical English garden, what you see is what you get—plants packed in there in volume but

not with much drama. And the American TV 'show-it-to-me' sensibility also stresses just the surface of things. In a Japanese garden, you're asked to get below the surface and to the essence of what it is saying."

The tablescapes that Wolf creates for his clients and for himself have a sense of composition and balance similar to the Japanese approach to flower arranging. "Diversity is the key—a delicate balance of different shapes, textures, scales, and provenance," he advises. "Make sure you have something high, something medium, and something low. It is the play of one form against another that gives strength to the composition."

above, left to right: The Cuban-born designer and photographer has several orchids in bloom at any given time. The photograph over the guest room sofa was taken by Vicente Wolf in Sikkim in the eastern Himalayas. The portrait of Oscar Levant is by Richard Avedon.

clockwise from right:
Bleached animal skulls and orchids make an arresting tablescape. African masks arrayed on an 18th-century Swedish table. Drawings on vellum by Robert Longo hang above a French limed-oak pool chaise. *opposite:* A teak Buddha from Thailand serenely shares space in the library hall with an orchid and a photograph of California dunesland by Edward Weston.

Flowers themselves make a space seem suddenly fresh and clean, the designer believes. "I love yellow flowers because they bring a sense of sunshine to a room," he says, "but when in doubt, white is always a good choice. And I like a bouquet to be made of just one type and color of flower—it makes more of an impact on a room."

Don't look for silk flowers or dried flowers in a room designed by Vicente Wolf, however. "For me, only fresh flowers embody a moment in time. You enjoy them in each stage from bud to blossom, and then they are gone. The fact that they are ephemeral is part of their beauty."

A Potter for All Seasons

Art is a continuous process. However new the circumstances may be, it is virtually impossible to create a work of art without antecedents.

—GEOFFREY AND SUSAN JELLICOE, *The Landscape of Man* (1975)

Like gardeners, potters work with the earth. In the case of Guy Wolff, America's foremost artist in gardening pots, that earth consists of red clay from deposits in Ohio, sand that is mined in Mystic, Connecticut, and a Missouri natural resource known as "fire clay," which the potter says lends strength to the body of the finished pot.

The special combination of ingredients aside, it is Wolff's mastery of the process of throwing a pot, combining hand speed with consummate skill and precision, along with his appreciation for the age-old traditions and designs of "pots with a purpose," that has earned him a broad following among amateur and professional gardeners in this country and abroad. Sturbridge Village in Massachusetts and Mystic Seaport in Connecticut are among the institutions that have incorporated his handiwork into their historical re-creations. He has made pots for Monticello in Charlottesville, Virginia; for Colonial Williamsburg, also in Virginia; the Historic Bartram's Garden in Philadelphia; and the New York Botanical Garden, and his work is featured in the collections of the American Ceramic Society's Museum of Ceramics, the Atlanta

opposite: Guy Wolff's round kiln, built in 1980, is a direct descendant of the workhorse kiln of the 19th-century English pottery industry. The kiln reaches a temperature of 2,500 degrees Fahrenheit when fully fired.

right and below: The showroom at Wolff Pottery in Litchfield County, Connecticut, offers a wide range of 18th- and 19th-century English and American designs, personally adapted by the master potter.

History Center, the Japanese Folk Craft Museum in Tokyo, and the Mingei International Museum in San Diego. A few years ago, always aware of his historical antecedents, and inspired by an 1801 portrait in the National Gallery by Rembrandt Peale, showing a 19th-century "Roped Full

Pot," which happened to contain the first geranium to come to America, Wolff created special pots and donated them to the White House Garden.

In contrast to the bustle and sophistica-tion of the nation's capital, Wolff lives and works in a thoroughly rustic environment, his pottery perched on a hill in the rural Woodville section of Washington, Connecticut. The slightly ramshackle building was erected in the 1920s to house a pet donkey belonging to the actress Mary Pickford, who was renting a summer place nearby at the time. The front room serves as a display area for his wares, all sized and contoured according to the plant they will host.

"The flower pot is a secondary actor," says Guy, downplaying the beauty of his designs in favor of function. "The number one thing is to disappear. A topiary pot should say, 'Look up there.'"

Wolff's tall, slender containers provide a sound base for topiaries or deep-rooted herbs such as bay laurel, while squat containers are designed to hold bulbs or shallow-rooted annuals. The color of the clay also serves a purpose for gardeners. Pots in light clay keep roots cool in the summer, while darker surfaces help retain heat on cold windowsills in winter.

Wolff pursues a craft with ancient roots. In the Middle East, pots have been thrown on the wheel for five thousand years. Italian potters mastered a coiling technique for making large terra-cotta pots without use of the wheel, introducing ornamental swags and other decorative touches to their designs. The decorative Italian style was introduced to England during the Renaissance, but an 18th-century gardening revolution, led by the

landscaping designs of Capability Brown, rejected the fancy in flower pot design in favor of utility and simplicity, and that has remained the English style.

"The pots I make are 18th- and 19th-century English and American designs that I have adapted for one reason or another," Guy says, citing the influence of his father, Robert J. Wolff, an abstract painter who cofounded the Chicago School of Design and later chaired the art department at Brooklyn College. "My father once wrote, 'Tradition is not a form to be imitated, but the discipline that gives integrity to the new.' That sums up what I'm trying to do."

Guy first became interested in pottery while attending High Mowing School in Wilton, New Hampshire. His interest

above: The finishing touches that give Wolff pots their elegance and integrity include scored lines, braiding, and a variety of styles for the rims of the vessels. *overleaf:* A batch of white Long Toms, inspired by a style popular with gardeners in Victorian England, made by Guy Wolff's son, Ben.

above: Guy Wolff often draws inspiration for current projects from his collection of antique pots, many of them gifts to him from friends and admirers in the gardening world.

deepened after spending a summer working at the Jugtown Pottery in Seagrove, North Carolina, operated by the Owens family since the 1720s. "I thought that was wonderful," he recalls. "Here was a family that had a tradition all its own and was following it without being totally bound by it. Since then, I've always welcomed the chance to be with potteries that have a 'family memory' of the craft going back a hundred years or more."

Determined to learn his craft through contact with artisans rather than by the academic track, Wolff hit the road for sev-

eral years. After stints at potteries in Wales, including one with kilns still standing from the 1600s, he found inspiration at the cobblestone-floored Wetheriggs Pottery near Penrith in Cumbria in the north of England, a national industrial monument that turned out its first piece in 1858. In Barnstable, England, he rubbed shoulders with a renowned potter named Frank Parsley, who had thrown pots for the garden of the Queen Mother herself. Parsley gave him one of his own metal shaping tools, called a potter's rib, which Wolff still uses every day.

Under the old guild system in Britain, apprentices practiced for seven and a half years before they were considered craftsmen. Guy followed this with seven and a half years in journeymanship before finally earning master potter status.

Today, Wolff throws about 125 tons of wet clay a year on his wheel, producing pots ranging in size from 2 inches high to 20 inches high, in shape from lean Long Toms to broad urns. He throws about 600 pounds of clay daily, which he considers below average. "A really good potter will do more than a thousand pounds a day," he notes. "If conditions are favorable, some veteran potters could turn out five pots a minute."

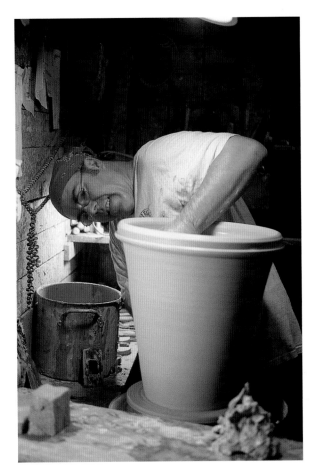

Even if his productivity doubled, Guy would be unlikely to meet the demand for his work. Upscale garden stores, nurseries, and mail-order houses carry his pots, but availability changes from season to season, in part because Wolff is very particular about the quality and integrity of the outlets in which his work is sold. Wolff has partnered with firms to design lines of pottery which are produced in workshops in Italy, Honduras, and the United States. The only sure way to secure a signed piece of his pottery and, more to the point, to see a superb craftsman in action, is simply to make the journey to Woodville.

"You can't imagine how much I love what I'm doing," Guy will tell a visitor as he lifts a wall of clay up and out from his wheel in the dusty room in the back of his shop. Romantic as that assertion may sound, there is another side to living an artist's life. "When people walk in and say, 'Oh, I wish I had your lifestyle,' I always say, 'I wish I had your medical insurance.'"

Guy Wolff is an artist grounded, like his pottery, in the real world.

clockwise from above left: Guy Wolff performing his "dance of the hands," as garden writer Tovah Martin has described it. His seal of approval is on every pot. Wolff prepares to deliver a shipment of finished pots.

Taking the High Ground

*Pictures, paints, pots, palettes—all the P's of a painter...
and inspiration pouring in with the happy sunshine.*

—RUTH R. BLODGETT, *The House Beautiful* (1918)

Artist Patricia Geary Johnson's two-and-a-half-acre hanging garden of delights, part of aptly named Rolling Hills in Southern California, has been a work in progress ever since the first plantings went in more than three decades ago.

An award-winning watercolorist with an unusual specialty as one of the U.S. Navy's few "combat artists," Johnson practices a firm, no-nonsense form of horticulture, not unlike the discipline she relies on to render dramatic wartime scenes of naval vessels in action.

"If a plant isn't developing right," she says, "I pull it out like a weed. I don't have room to maintain a plant hospital. I'm not afraid to say, 'This has got to go.'"

The steep terrain of the homesite, at 1,100 feet, overlooking the dramatic Rancho Palos Verdes peninsula and offering an 180-degree view of the Pacific Ocean, posed a daunting challenge when gardens were first undertaken here in 1974. Johnson turned to noted landscape designer Ruth Shellhorn to lay out the basic structure for the terrain. Pathways and stairs were engineered to make the hillside location accessible, with strategically placed benches to provide both prospect and respite.

"Ruth was of the old school of landscape design," Johnson recalls, "preferring everything to be green. Naturally, as a painter, I kept looking for opportunities to

opposite: With lemons on the right and kumquats on the left, the orchard path in Patricia Johnson's steeply pitched garden is bordered by miniature orange daylilies and leads into plantings of flax and white ginger.

above: In a formal garden near the house are some fifty hybrid tea roses, underplanted with blue fescue. *right:* The floribunda rose 'Trumpeter' flourishes on the southwest hillside facing the ocean, along with society garlic, ground morning glory, pensemon, and, at the top, lavender 'Goodwin Creek'.

add color." In time she enlisted the services of Pomona landscape designer John Greenlee, who was best known for his knowledge and use of ornamental grasses and roses. Today a mass of shrub roses, including the varieties 'Iceberg', 'Bonica', 'Pink Mediland', and 'The Fairy', climb the front slope from the driveway. Nearby, a formal hybrid tea rose garden, some 50 plants with an undercarpet of blue fescue, along with another 250 roses of other varieties elsewhere on the property, provide a

nearly year-round source of cut flowers for the house.

Concentrations of color are found, one after another, by design, as one travels the pathway away from the house. A vein of yellow and gold streams up the hill along the south slope, comprising poker and marmalade plants, Matilija poppies, perennial marigolds, and variegated pampas grasses. Elsewhere, a red room in the garden, containing succulents, dahlias, azaleas, and camellias, directs the eye to the coastline and spectacular sunsets. A slope of blue shore juniper leads into a lavender-and-blue room filled with society garlic, penstemon, trailing rosemary, and ground morning glory vines. *Stipa gigantea* punctuates the slope with its wispy tall flower spikes responding to the slightest breeze.

Through a thicket of macadamia nut trees, the path takes the visitor back uphill to the north side of the house. Here a checkered-bark ornamental pear provides dappled shade for begonias, bromeliads, camellias, and ferns.

Other visual themes in the Johnson garden reflect other aspects of the California experience. The state's agricultural largesse immediately comes to mind as one walks through the heavily fruited mixed orchard, on a slope below the yellow room, of cherimoya, apricot, avocado, fig, persimmon, and peach. Elsewhere, the influence of the Far East is felt in the presence of a dozen bonsai, beautifully sculpted by Japanese master gardeners, and a sitting area in the back of the house furnished with Chinese lanterns and chimes.

below: The view of the Pacific Ocean over wildflowers and ornamental grasses that move in the slightest breeze never ceases to enthrall.

Johnson, who has traveled in Japan and China, admires "the simplicity of the line in really good Oriental art." She herself studied ikebana for nine years, not so much to master that highly structured style of arranging flowers, as to improve her understanding of the physical characteristics of the flowers themselves, to be able to draw them better.

Professionally, Patricia has painted many subjects besides flowers and landscapes, including an "Irish Castles" series that was commissioned by the Irish Tourist Board, but her fame rests in her work for the Navy, and her paintings are currently displayed on U.S. Navy ships, in U.S. Naval installations and museums, and in private collections.

Johnson entered into her chosen field

not entirely by chance. Her father, Ted Geary, was one of America's most respected designers of small racing boats, sailboats, and yachts, including a 100-foot-long luxury yacht for the actor John Barrymore. During World War II, he designed minesweepers and other warships for the Navy. Sadly, Geary did not live to see his daughter's career blossom. Nevertheless, with intimate experience of ships in her family background, Patricia decided to hone the art skills she had learned at Stanford University by drawing boats, having decided that, after the human figure, boats are the most challenging subjects to draw.

"After I finished my education, I realized I wanted to draw things well, and having grown up along the coast, it was

natural for me just to go down to the sea and start drawing boats," she recalls. "Then one day, when I was painting someone's yacht or fishing boat, I saw a Navy ship go by in the distance. It was a destroyer that had just been commissioned with all its flags flying and its firearms on high-alert, and I thought, 'Wow, if I could ever do that, I think I'll be good.'"

Johnson got herself onto Navy installations, and eventually was introduced to Arthur Beaumont, a famous naval combat artist, with whom she began studying. One thing led to another, she says, and the Navy began to recognize her work. She did face gender-related obstacles in the early days and for a time she signed her paintings "Pat Johnson" just to keep a low profile.

"The old-timers in the Navy didn't think females could paint," she relates. "I couldn't go out overnight on a ship, of course—it was just forbidden. But with women sailors stationed aboard ships today, that is no longer a problem."

The painting technique Johnson has mastered is pure transparent watercolor, what she calls "wet into wet with dry brush accent." Like her gardens, her paintings are radiantly alive, and those depicting ships, especially, surely would have made her father proud.

opposite: A closeup of the long-blooming pincushion (*Leucospermum cordifolium*) in Patricia Johnson's "yellow room."

clockwise from above: A river of succulents is flanked by miniature roses, pink geraniums, blue fescue, and purple verbena on one side and by bougainvillea on the other. A closeup of succulents. The "yellow room" on a south-facing slope features pincushion, poker plant, perennial marigold, and variegated yucca and pampas grass.

EXCURSION: Lotusland

At the heart of gardening there may need to be a belief in the miraculous.

—MIRABEL OSLER, *A Gentle Plea for Chaos* (1989)

immensity of the Infinite," wrote Ganna Walska, in her 1943 autobiography, *Always Room
at the Top,* a book described by one critic as
"not overly concerned with distinguishing
between fact and fiction." Lotusland, the
unconventional but relentlessly seductive
melange of gardens that Walska created on
an old thirty-seven-acre estate in Montecito,
California, 90 miles north of Los Angeles, over
a period of four decades, is not entirely to be
believed, either.

But the gardens make you happy.

"She gave us a wonderland, marvelous
plants, plants you will see nowhere else,"
says Virginia Hayes, curator of the nonprofit
group that has run Lotusland since its founder
died in 1984, at the age of ninety-seven. "You
could talk about almost anything in the whole
realm of botany and find an illustration here.
But Ganna Walska was not your average
backyard gardener," she adds. "Her design
ideas and choice of plants weren't normal.
She had a different vision from most of us."

That vision was shaped by Walska's early
up-and-down career as an opera singer (the
low point coming one night when a theater
audience threw vegetables at her for failing to
sing on key), a passionate but ultimately luck-
less love life, and, perhaps most important, a
lifelong spiritual quest for what was true and
good about life itself, with gardening at the
heart of it.

Born Hanna Puacz in Czarist Poland in
1887, she went to St. Petersburg in her teens,
married a Russian count, began to sing professionally, and invented a more sibilant name
for herself, combining Polish words for
"graceful" and "waltz" to emerge as Madame
Ganna Walska. Although never achieving diva
status in the opera world, Walska possessed
a sensual, charismatic beauty that never
failed to attract the eye of future husbands
and society page editors, "each liaison gush-
ingly chronicled in headlines," as Edwin
Kiester Jr. wrote in *Smithsonian* magazine.
"With her raven hair, patrician profile, swan-
like neck and ample bosom atop a trim figure,
she was quickly acknowledged as a great
beauty." The spoils from a total of six mar-
riages, all but one of them to wealthy men,
included stately homes in Paris and Manhattan, a French château, even her own theater,
also in Paris, and multiple lifelong alimony
arrangements.

It was in 1941 that the man who would
become her sixth husband, a Tibetan scholar
and limber-limbed yogi named Theos
Bernard, persuaded Walska to buy the Montecito property, then known as Cuesta Linda.
Renaming the place Tibetland, Ganna and
Theos hoped to make Cuesta Linda a center
for Eastern mysticism—a kind of precursor of
the now famous Esalen Institute that came
into being many years later, farther up the
coast at Big Sur—but divorce No. 6 in 1946
put an end to that dream. This time, renaming
the place Lotusland (after the lotus flowers
she found growing in a pond on her land) for
good, Madame threw herself into gardening,
and never looked back.

below: In the 1950s, Ganna Walska personally supervised the conversion of a swimming pool into her Water Garden, filling it with lotuses, one of the oldest flowering plant species still in existence.

Although she called herself head gardener at Lotusland, Walska had no horticultural training. She made no effort to learn the Latin names for her exotic specimens, calling the New World desert plants on one side of the driveway "the cactus," and the African euphorbias on the other side "the *other* cactus."

"She wasn't a plant person in that sense," Hayes notes. "She wasn't interested in the names, only how things looked."

The estate house at Lotusland is an 8,000-square-foot pink stucco Mediterranean edifice built in 1919. Today, thanks to Walska's idea about how things should look, the main entry welcomes and at the same time menaces visitors with 30-foot-high succulent trees, their irregular branches sprawling to the ground like the arms of an octopus, and a collection of golden barrel cacti, spiny ottoman shapes dubbed mother-in-law seats for the lack of comfort they promise.

One of the gardening mantras of "Madame," as everyone on staff addressed her, was "More is better." In preparation for a visit from the prestigious Palm Society, she trucked in more than a hundred full-size palms to plant at the last minute, to make sure she had enough varieties to satisfy those she once described as "the palm nuts." Across the gravel driveway from the house is a miniature forest of closely planted dragon trees with a path that leads from a fern garden to a cactus garden, two of more than twenty garden rooms on the estate, each intriguing in its own way. The Aloe Garden with more than 170 species is set off by a crescent pool, with tufa stone islands and fountains crafted from giant South Pacific clam shells. The sunken Theatre Garden is populated with whimsical carved stone grotesques taken from the grounds of her French château. A garden of cycads, which cost more than a million dollars to assemble, contains more than four hundred of these prehistoric plants, resembling small palm trees but more closely related to the pine family, some of them extremely rare.

In 1971, to help pay for her cycads, Walska raised money by auctioning off some of her world-class jewelry collection, including diamonds, emeralds, and rubies, two tiaras, and a heart-shaped diamond ring, which alone fetched $105,000. Her five-acre Japanese Garden was another major investment. It is planted with flowering cherry trees, bonsai shrubs, black pine, maples, camellias, azaleas, and nandina, or heavenly bamboo, as well as other visual delights, such as a number of Japanese lanterns and an authentic Shinto shrine nestled among Japanese cedar trees. The garden's pond, lush with lotuses and water lilies, draws a wide variety of wild birds, including snowy and great egrets, green and great blue herons, wood ducks, black phoebes, and belted kingfishers. Turtles are frequently seen sunning themselves on the rocks near the bronze crane sculptures installed in the pond.

Madame was notoriously difficult to work for and her views on gardening sometimes made it hard for her staff to get things done efficiently. She had a high tolerance for

opposite: Dozens of gardens on Ganna Walska's 37-acre estate in Montecito still bear her signature style, emphasizing the whimsical and often flamboyant use of plants and garden ornaments, such as the lemon arbor running through the Fruit Orchard; she brought grotesque carved stone figures from her French estate to lend their unique personality to her outdoor Theatre Garden.

EXCURSION

below: Ganna Walksa in the 1920s, when she had already achieved celebrity status as an international beauty. *opposite, above:* Numerous varieties of cacti, including the tall old man cactus, line the driveway leading to the main house at Lotusland. *opposite, below:* The Horticultural Clock, complete with signs of the zodiac, was created for Ganna Walska by Santa Barbara landscape designer Ralph Stevens; in the background is the Topiary Garden.

weeds, for example, and a low tolerance for anything with a motor, such as the power tools that make pruning and trimming easier tasks. She did not hesitate to consult with the best landscape architects she could find to help her design and build new gardens over the years, but sometimes she ran through designers as fast as she had run through husbands. She hired a noted design firm to work on the Japanese Garden, but was so annoyed with the plans they presented that she threw them on the ground and stalked off. Later she gave the job to Frank Fujii, a staff gardener, and Oswald da Ros, a stonemason, and their collaboration was a great success. Fujii, who spent the next thirty years working on the Japanese Garden, remembers Madame as a woman with definite opinions but also a willingness to compromise. She could fly off the handle at a moment's notice, but "if she was

wrong about something, she'd apologize," he says. "She had a big heart."

In the years since Ganna Walska's death, the Lotusland Foundation has not been idle. In 1995, the gardens developed a sustainable garden program without dependence on chemicals of any kind. Huge compost heaps with citizen armies of earthworms yield nutritious mulch, which along with wood chips is spread in all areas of the garden. Plants are sprayed regularly with "compost tea"—a liquid concoction with beneficial organisms. New collections of native plants that attract "good-guy" insects provide a steady flow of natural predators to attack unwanted larvae and other pests.

More recently, hundreds of cactus specimens, many more than 45 feet tall, from a San Diego garden that measured 350 feet long and 80 feet deep, were moved to a brand-new garden area at Lotusland. Merritt S. Dunlap picked Lotusland to receive his vast collection, which he started in 1929, largely because of Dunlap's personal affection and admiration for Walska that began with his first visit to Lotusland in 1966.

"I think the main attraction in this garden is still Ganna Walska," says Lotusland curator Virginia Hayes. "It is one woman's creation, an interesting woman, a many-sided woman. Even for those of us here, she remains mysterious, an unknown quantity."

THE GARDENER'S LIFE

Inspired Plantsmen, Passionate Collectors, and Singular Visions in the World of Gardening

RESOURCES

PLANTSMEN

Rose Story Farm
Carpinteria, CA 93013
(866) 566-4885
www.rosestoryfarm.com
More than 100 varieties of antique, shrub, and old
hybrid tea roses, almost all pre-1950, with unusual
shapes, colors, and fragrances; gift shop with
gardening equipment for rose enthusiasts.

Roger's Gardens
2301 San Joaquin Hills Rd.
Corona del Mar, CA 92625
(949) 640-5800 (direct)
(949) 721-2100 (general information)
www.Rogersgardens.com
One of the largest garden centers in Southern
California, with numerous display gardens; gift and
book store; garden tools and furnishings; ongoing
lecture series on gardening and related subjects.

Gilberties Herb Gardens
7 Sylvan La.
Westport, CT 06880
(203) 227-4175
www.gilbertiesherbs.com
Herbal plants and products, vegetable plants,
flowering annuals and perennials, vegetables; gift shop;
gardening and crafts programs.

Comstock, Ferre & Co.
263 Main St.
Wethersfield, CT 06109
(800) 733-3773
www.comstockferre.com
Oldest continuously operating seed company in the
U.S.; complete garden center with seeds, herb and
vegetable plants, flowering annuals, perennials, and
vines.

Cricket Hill Garden
670 Walnut Hill Rd.
Thomaston, CT 06787
(860) 283-1042
www.treepeony.com
More than 300 varieties of Chinese tree peonies and
herbaceous peonies in a 6-acre garden called Peony
Heaven. (Prime blooming time from mid-May until
about June 10.) Catalogs available—sign up on
website.

Allen Haskell Landscape Services and Garden Center
787 Shawmut Ave.
New Bedford, MA 02746
(508) 993-9046
Rare and unusual plants in award-winning display
gardens, including a vast collection of indoor and
outdoor topiaries.

ATTRACTIONS

CALIFORNIA

Mission San Juan Capistrano
31414 El Camino Real
San Juan Capistrano, CA 92675
(949) 234-1300
www.missionsjc.com
Founded in 1776, the seventh in the California
mission chain and the centerpiece of the town's
historic district features a wide variety of fountains
and garden landscapes.

Ganna Walska Lotusland
695 Ashley Rd.
Santa Barbara, CA 93108
(805) 969-9990 (reservation office Mon.–Fri.
9 A.M.–noon)
www.lotusland.org
Open for docent-led 2-hour walking tours, mid-
February through mid-November, Wednesday through
Saturday, 10 A.M. or 1:30 P.M. All visitors must have
advance phone reservations.

Santa Barbara Farmer's Market
Santa Barbara, CA
Conducted five days a week at various locations, year
round, rain or shine.
(805) 962-5354
www.farmersmarket.org

Santa Monica Airport Flea Market
Santa Monica, CA
Held fourth Sunday of every month.
(323) 933-2511

Bell Gardens Farm
30841 Cole Grade Rd.
P.O. Box 2450
Valley Center, CA 92082
(760) 749-6297
www.bellgardensfarm.com
Nonprofit agricultural center with seasonal produce
market, farm-related classes and workshops, on 115
acres of cultivated fields, creek beds, walking trails,
and lawns for picnics.

ILLINOIS

Chicago Botanic Garden
1000 Lake Cook Rd.
Glencoe, IL
Antiques & Garden Fair
Held in April.
(847) 835-5440
www.chicagobotanic.org/antiques

MASSACHUSETTS

Brimfield Outdoor Antiques & Collectibles Shows
Brimfield, MA
Conducted in May, July, and September.
(413) 283-2418
www.quaboag.com

Glass Flowers
Harvard Museum of Natural History
26 Oxford St.
Cambridge, MA 02138
(617) 495-2566
The Ware Collection of Glass Models of Plants
contains approximately 3,000 models, representing
more than 830 species, each with a scientifically
accurate, life-size model and magnified parts.

Massachusetts Horticultural Society
900 Washington St.
Wellesley, MA 02482
(617) 933-4935
www.masshort.org
Located in new quarters, since 2001, on the 36-acre
Elm Bank Estate with display gardens, greenhouses,
education center, gift shop, and library containing
more than 50,000 books, periodicals, and seed
catalogs, as well as a collection of 1,200 early
19th- and 20th-century botanical prints.

NEW YORK

Hamptons Spring Garden Antiques Show & Sale
Bridgehampton, NY
Held in June.

Gramercy Garden Antiques Show
New York, NY
Held in February.
(212) 255-0020
www.stellashows.com

New York Botanical Garden
The Bronx, NY
Antique Garden Furniture Show & Sale
Held in April or May.
(718) 817-8700
www.nybg.org

PENNSYLVANIA

Hunt Institute for Botanical Documentation
Carnegie Mellon University
Pittsburgh, PA 15213-3890
(412) 268-2434
http://huntbot.andrew.cmu.edu
Collection of botanical art, literature, and archival
materials, including some 30,000 individual
watercolors, drawings, and prints.

RHODE ISLAND

Newport Flower Show
c/o The Preservation Society of Newport County
424 Bellevue Ave.
Newport, RI 02840
(401) 847-1000, ext. 150
www.NewportFlowerShow.org

TEXAS

Lady Bird Johnson Wildflower Center
4801 La Crosse Ave.
Austin, TX 78739-1702
(512) 292-4200
www.wildflower.org
Gardens and grounds with more than 400 species of
grasses, shrubs, trees, and wildflowers native to central
Texas; courses, workshops, lectures; gift shop, café.

Antique Rose Emporium
G. Michael Shoup, founder and owner
9300 Lueckemeyer Rd.
Brenham, TX 77833
(800) 441-0002
www.weAREroses.com
Hundreds of varieties of old garden roses, as well as
other perennial plants; numerous display gardens.

Round Top Antiques Fair
Emma Lee Turney, founder and manager
P.O. Box 821289
Houston, TX 77282-1289
(281) 493-5501
www.roundtopantiquesfair.com
Annual antiques and folk art show, first full weekends
in April and October.

McAshan Herb Gardens at Festival Hill
Madalene Hill, garden curator
Gwen Barclay, director of food service
P.O. Box 89
Round Top, TX 78954-0089
(979) 249-5283
gwenbarclay_herbs@hotmail.com
Spring events include guided tours of gardens,
luncheons, lectures, and seminars.

Garden Antique Shops, Dealers, Collectors, Craftsmen

CALIFORNIA

Nicola Wagner
P.O. Box 1268
Aptos, CA 95003
(831) 689-9227
www.members.aol.com/nmfiggis
Nineteenth-century botanical prints, engravings, and
lithographs.

Lyons Ltd. Antique Prints
10 Town & Country Village
(El Camino and Embarcadero)
Palo Alto, CA 94301
(650) 325-9010
www.LyonsLtd.com
Original engravings, etchings, and lithographs, since
1968.

Blue Canoe
2902 Halladay
Santa Ana, CA 92705
(714) 708-3658
Architectural antiques and eclectic furnishings for
home and garden.

Urban Country
218 Main St.
Venice, CA 90291
(310) 315-1927
info@urbancountryantiques.com
Antique garden, painted furniture, and folk art.

CONNECTICUT

R. T. Facts
Greg and Natalie Randall
Old Town Hall
22 S. Main St.
Kent, CT 06757
(860) 927-1700
www.rtfacts.com
Garden and architectural antiques.

G. Wolff & Sons
305 Litchfield Tpk.
New Preston, CT 06777
(860) 868-2858
gwolff@javanet.com
Horticultural and traditional pottery.

Circa Antiques
11 Riverside Ave.
Westport, CT 06880
(203) 222-8642
European antiques, accessories, and garden ornaments.

GEORGIA

A. Tyner Antiques
200 Bennett St. NW
Lower Level
Atlanta, GA 30309
(404) 758-7763 (warehouse)
(404) 367-4484 (retail)
www.swedishantiques.biz
Botanical prints, seed bottles, and other garden
antiques and folk art; Swedish furniture.

ILLINOIS

The Finnegan Gallery
2030 N. Mohawk
Chicago, IL 60614
(312) 951-6858
FinneganGallery@earthlink.net
By appointment.

Salvage One
1840 W. Hubbard
Chicago, IL 60622
(312) 733-0098

Trellis & Trugs
1009 Green Bay Rd.
Winnetka, IL 60093
(847) 784-6910
Garden antiques and unique garden ornaments.

LOUISIANA

Nest
Annie McClure, showing at
Marburger Farm Antique Show,
Round Top, TX
(318) 869-1220
nest@sport.rr.com
Naturalists' collections, botanical specimens, rural
furniture, and farm artifacts.

MAINE

Riverbank Antiques
1755 Post Rd./U.S. Route 1
Wells, ME 04090
(207) 646-6314

The Spire Trellis
89 Tuell Town Rd.
West Paris, ME 04289
(877) 674-5959
www.spiretrellis.com
3½- to 4½-foot spire-shaped trellises of cedar with oak
hoop and brass hardware; also corset-type trellises.

Marston House Antiques/Bed & Breakfast
101 Main St.
Wiscasset, ME 04578
(207) 882-6010
www.marstonhouse.com

MASSACHUSETTS

The Reel Lawn Mower
James B. Ricci
30 N. Farms Rd.
Haydenville, MA 01039-9724
(413) 268-7863
jricci@reellawnmower.com
19th- and early-20th-century hand, horse, and motor
mowers, as well as catalogs, ephemera, literature, and
photographs; by appointment.

Cut It Out
326 Old Stockbridge Rd.
Lenox, MA 01240
(413) 637-0400
www.heycutitout.com
Functional garden art handmade with natural
ingredients by Janice Shields, including arbors,
trellises, gates, benches, chairs, and obelisks.

C. J. Sprong & Co.
300 Pleasant St.
Northampton, MA 01060
(413) 584-7440
www.cjsprong.com
Garden furniture, pots, statuary, *tuteurs,* trellises,
arbors.

New England Stoneworks
9 Butler Pl.
Northampton, MA 01060
(413) 586-7496
ytte@rcn.com
Original work by sculptor Tim de Christopher in
limestone, marble, granite, sandstone, slate, bronze,
and steel; studio visits by appointment.

New England Garden Ornaments
38 East Brookfield Rd.
North Brookfield, MA 01535
(508) 867-4474
www.negardenornaments.com
Imported English garden ornaments including cast
stone, lead, granite troughs, terra cotta, cast iron,
armillary sundials, garden animals, and wall plaques.

Campo de' Fiori
Route 7
Sheffield, MA 01257
(413) 528-9180
www.campodefiori.com
Garden furniture and objects, European terra cotta,
French and Italian wire, hand-carved wood, stone urns
and planters, wrought iron, and hand-hammered
copper.

Z Studio
4 Look St.
Vineyard Haven, MA 02568
(508) 696-7799
purplefence@mindspring.com
Botanical collages by Peggy Turner Zablotny.

Debra Queen
Worcester, MA
(508) 991-3208
Vintage garden accessories including furniture, English
terra cotta, tools, architectural elements, and old vases
and flower pots; by appointment.

MICHIGAN

Celtic Garden Imports
P.O. Box 8038
Ann Arbor, MI 48107
(734) 997-9499
www.celticgardenimports.com
Architectural and farm salvage from Ireland, staddle
stones, urns, troughs, garden ornaments.

Worden Antiques & Select Objects
P.O. Box 306
Burr Oak, MI 49030
(269) 489-5311
Garden antiques and architectural remnants; by
appointment only.

NEW HAMPSHIRE

Landscape Books
Box 483
Exeter, NH 03833
(603) 964-9333
landscapebooks@aol.com
Vintage garden books; catalog available.

Dennis & Dad Antiques
33 NH Route 119 East
Fitzwilliam, NH 03477
(603) 585-9479
berard@top.monad.net
18th- and 19th-century English pottery, including
Staffordshire transferware and figures, ABC plates and
mugs, children's sets, Gaudy Welsh, yellowware, Leeds
pottery, creamware, and other antique accessories.

Sugarplum Antiques
Anne Rowe
242 U.S. Route 4
Wilmot, NH 03287
(603) 768-3925
English and European urns, vases, obelisks, fountains,
arbors, benches, sundials, wall sinks, staddle stones,
wheelbarrows, and sundry other small garden
furnishings, tools, and ornaments.

NEW JERSEY

Danielle Ann Millican
154 Summit Rd.
Florham Park, NJ 07932
(973) 360-0978
www.DanielleAnnMillican.com
16th- to 19th-century woodcuts, engravings,
lithographs; antique prints depicting natural history
and world exploration; by appointment or chance.

Elisabeth Woodburn Books
Box 398
Hopewell, NJ 08525
(609) 466-0522
www.woodburnbooks.com
Vintage garden books; free catalog on request.

NEW YORK

Glenn Horowitz Bookseller
87 Newtown La.
East Hampton, NY 11937
(631) 324-5511
Vintage garden books.

Barbara Israel Garden Antiques
Katonah, NY
(212) 744-6281
www.bi-gardenantiques.com
Antique garden ornaments and furniture from Europe
and America.

Bonni Benrubi Gallery
52 East 76th Street
New York, NY 10021
(212) 517-3766
www.bonnibenrubi.com
Works of contemporary artists and photographers,
including Judith McMillan.

Canyan Antiques
Ani Antreasyan
9 E. 97th St.
New York, NY 10029
(212) 722-5342
www.aniancientstone.com

Judith and James Milne
506 E. 74th St.
New York, NY 10021
(212) 472-0107
www.milneantiques.com
Antique garden ornaments and American folk art.

Olde Good Things
124 W. 24th St.
New York, NY 10011
(212) 989-8401
www.oldegoodthings.com
Architectural elements, statues, garden furniture.

Stubbs Books & Prints
153 E. 70th St.
New York, NY 10021
(212) 772-3120
Vintage garden books.

Ursus Books and Prints
981 Madison Ave.
New York, NY 10021
(212) 772-8787
www.ursusbooks.com
Botanical books, prints, and paintings.

Winter Works on Paper
160 Fifth Ave., Room 718
New York, NY 10010
www.winterworksonpaper.com
Art photography, original prints, botanical specimens, and nature prints. By appointment.

PENNSYLVANIA

Gardenium
P.O. Box 64
Newtown Square, PA 19073
(610) 891-9355
www.GARDENIUM.com
Consortium of artists specializing in furniture, gates and fences, fountains, ornament, and sculpture for the landscaped garden.

Flotsam + Jetsam
Meltem Birey
149 N. Third St.
Philadelphia, PA 19106
(215) 351-9914
Interior design, home and garden furnishings.

RHODE ISLAND

Owl's Head Garden Products
P.O. Box 1737
East Greenwich, RI 02818
(401) 885-4847
www.owlshead.safeshopper.com
Reproduction cast-iron Victorian planters and garden accessories.

Richard Kazarian Antiques
9 Montgomery St.
Pawtucket, RI 02860
(401) 724-0175

TEXAS

Good & Co.
Suzy Romeke
248 S. Main St.
Boerne, TX 78006
(830) 249-6101
Cottage antiques for home and garden, fountains, statuary, pottery, furniture.

Agnes R. Strauss
Wilde Weedz
1146 Kveton Rd.
Cat Spring, TX 78933
(979) 732-6012
Dried flowers, unique gourds, hooked rugs, and country garden accessories; by appointment.

Harmon Antiques & Design
I-30 & CR 4113
Campbell, TX 75422
(903) 454-4831
MCHarmon@kayote.com
Decorative garden antiques.

Lynette G. Proler
Proler Garden Antiques, Inc.
528 Palisades Dr. #501
Pacific Palisades, CA 90272
(310) 459-0477
info@garden-antiques.com
www.garden-antiques.com
European antiques and custom-designed stone and
marble garden ornaments.

Thompson Hanson
3600 W. Alabama
Houston, TX 77027
(713) 661-9500
Garden pots, statuary, architectural elements.

Harold Hollis
21309 C.R. 456
Normangee, TX 77871
(936) 396-1246
Country decorative arts, vintage Western and
Mexican, including furniture, pottery, textiles, baskets,
paintings, folk art, whimsy, and garden-related
accessories.

VERMONT

High Beams
Route 5
Sutton, VT 05867
(802) 467-3943
www.highbeams.com
Handmade mica, styrene, and goat-skin parchment
lampshades with dried botanical decorations and bases
of beaten copper or brass.

WASHINGTON

Hinck & Wall
(formerly Anchor & Dolphin Books)
P.O. Box 1232
Edmonds, WA 98020
Vintage books on garden history, landscape
architecture, applied and decorative arts.

REFERENCES

The Avant Gardener
Horticultural Data Processors
Box 489
New York, NY 10028
Monthly newsletter about the world of horticulture, with information on plant sources and news and views of trends and developments in all categories of gardening. Thomas Powell, editor and publisher; Betty Powell, executive editor.

The Garden Conservancy
P.O. Box 219
Cold Spring, NY 10516
(914) 265-2029
National garden preservation organization and sponsor of annual "open days" fund-raising program offering visits to hundreds of private gardens in Connecticut and in Westchester, Putnam, and Dutchess Counties and on Long Island in New York, eventually to include gardens throughout the United States.

Gardening by Mail
Tusker Press
P.O. Box 1338
Sebastopol, CA 95473
(707) 829-9189
A Tusker Press Book by Barbara J. Barton, published by Houghton Mifflin, this is a directory of mail-order resources for gardeners in the U.S. and Canada, including seed companies, nurseries, suppliers of all garden necessaries and ornaments, horticultural and plant societies, magazines, libraries, and a list of useful books on plants and gardening. (If out of print, copies may be obtained on the Internet via used-book websites such as www.amazon.com or www.alibris.com.)

The Garden Tourist
The Garden Tourist Press
330 W. 72nd St.
New York, NY 10023
A guide to garden tours, garden days, shows, and special events in the U.S., Canada, and abroad. (If out of print, copies may be obtained on the Internet via used-book websites such as www.amazon.com or www.alibris.com.)

The Garden Lover's Guide to the Northeast,
The Garden Lover's Guide to the South,
The Garden Lover's Guide to the Midwest,
and *The Garden Lover's Guide to the West*
Princeton Architectural Press
37 E. 7th St.
New York, NY 10003
(800) 722-6657
www.papress.com
Distributed by Chronicle Books
(212) 995-9620
www.pubeasy.com
Four comprehensive regional guides to hundreds of public and semiprivate gardens including maps and driving directions, contact data, and admission fees; illustrated with color photographs.

ACKNOWLEDGMENTS

We were helped along our winding garden path by too many people to mention here by name, but in our immediate area of western Massachusetts we would like to single out Jim Ricci, Beverly Duncan, and Mark Zenick of New Hope Farm; David Fisher of Natural Roots, a Community Supported Agriculture venture; Ellen Kaufmann of the Lavender & Herb Growers of Franklin County; the officers and staff of the Hillside Agricultural Society, sponsors of the Cummington Fair, a highlight of the summer in our hill towns; and Eric Nelson and Peg Sloan, neighbors with a green thumb and warm heart. Cheri Stark, along with the plants and people at Annie's, Bay State Perennials, Blue Meadow Farm, Nasami Farm, Mill River Farm, and a host of other resources in our area, helped make our own gardens look almost up to standard. In the Berkshires proper, we got help from Janice Shields, maker of rustic garden structures, and our friends and keen gardeners Julie Michaels and Pad Spence. Thanks also to John Peterson and Kathleen Sharkey of the Massachusetts Horticultural Society, Susan Rossi-Wilcox of Harvard's Museum of Natural History, repository of the remarkable Glass Flowers collection, and Allen C. Haskell, whose New Bedford garden center is a horticultural wonder.

Elsewhere in New England we owe a debt of gratitude to Anne and Garrett Rowe, Ann and Dennis Berard, Marie and Sal Gilbertie of Gilberties Herb Gardens, potter extraordinaire Guy Wolff, Pamela Peck of Comstock, Ferre & Co., Brenda Milkofsky of the Wethersfield Historical Society, Kasha and David Furman of Cricket Hill Garden, "Peony Heaven" by any other name, and Mrs. Samuel M. V. Hamilton, chairman of the 2001 Newport Flower Show, and Mary Beach, show manager.

Moving westward, we thank Judith McMillan, Karen and Doug Jimerson and Elvin McDonald, and Harold Hollis, for sharing their gardens and collections at their homes in, respectively, Ohio, Iowa, and Texas. Other Texas credits are due to Madalene Hill and Gwen Barclay of the McAshan Herb Gardens at Festival Hill, Round Top; Emma Lee Turney, whose twice-yearly antiques and folk art fair in Round Top is always a hit with gardeners looking for weathered adornments for their garden spaces; the volunteers at Bayou Bend in Houston; the friendly staff at the Lady Bird Johnson Wildflower Center in Austin; and G. Michael Shoup, owner of the Antique Rose Emporium in Brenham.

Our visits to some of California's most amazing gardens were made even more enjoyable by the warm hospitality of Danielle and Bill Hahn of Rose Story Farm, Ninetta and Gavin Herbert of La Casa Pacifica, Lew Whitney of Roger's Gardens, Bobby Webb and Michael Corbett, and Patricia Geary Johnson. We were also inspired by visits to the gardens of Mission San Juan Capistrano, Julia Rappaport in Santa Ana, Bell Gardens Farm in Valley Center, hydrangea grower Jim Hipple of Carpinteria, and the Santa Barbara Farmers Market, where we met mesclun pioneer Tom Shepherd and Julia Child on the same Saturday morning. Our thanks go to Deanna Hatch for arranging our visit to the nonpareil Lotusland of Ganna Walska in Santa Barbara. Above all, Electa Anderson made our trip to Southern California fruitful and fun.

Back on the East Coast, our sincere thanks to New Yorkers Abbie Zabar, David Winter, and Vicente Wolf, for letting us visit and photograph their extraordinary visions that pass for apartments, as well as John Romell of Merchant House and the volunteers at the Liz Christy Garden.

At Clarkson Potter, our gratitude extends to our editor, Lauren Shakely, and her assistant, Robecca Glover; Mark McCauslin and Joan Denman for copyediting and production; and creative director Marysarah Quinn and designer Dina Dell'Arciprete for the book's beautiful design.

INDEX

Note: Pages in *italics* refer to captions.